Fo

AP BC Calculus:
The Ultimate Guide

Over 550 Practice Problems

Vivek Raghuram and Baxter Thompson
First Edition

Published by Gift Of Logic, Inc.

http://www.giftoflogic.com/

FocusPrep™ is an imprint of Gift Of Logic, Inc.

ISBN-13: 978-1986642019

ISBN-10: 1986642011

March 2018

AP BC CALCULUS: THE ULTIMATE GUIDE

Chapter 1: Properties of Logarithmic Functions

Basic Logarithmic Properties, Log Solving, and Simplifying

Basic Logarithmic Properties

Basic Logarithmic Properties

Definition of a Logarithm	If $\log_a b = n$, then $a^n = b$
Sum of Logarithms	$\log(x) + \log(y) = \log(xy)$
Difference of Logarithms	$\log(x) - \log(y) = \log\left(\dfrac{x}{y}\right)$
Logarithmic Exponent Rule	$\log(x^n) = n \cdot \log(x)$
Natural Base Logarithm	$\log_e x = \ln(x)$
Logarithmic Base Change	$\log_a b = \dfrac{\log b}{\log a}$
Special Logarithmic Properties	$\log_a(1) = 0$ $\log_a(a) = 1$ $\log_a(a^n) = n$ $a^{\log_a(n)} = n$

1.1 Find the value of b in the equation $\log_2(b) = 4$

Using the definition of a logarithm, $2^4 = b$. Therefore the value of $b = 16$.

1.2 Simplify $\log(3x) + \log(y)$

The sum of two logarithmic functions is equal to logarithm of the product of the arguments, or the inner functions.

$$\log(3x) + \log(y) = \log(3xy)$$

1.3 Simplify $\log(x) - \log(2y)$

The difference of two logarithmic functions is equal to the logarithm of the quotient of the arguments.

$$\log(x) - \log(2y) = \log\left(\frac{x}{2y}\right)$$

1.4 Simplify $\log(x^3)$

Using the log exponent rule, we can bring down the exponent in front of the logarithmic function.

$$\log(x^3) = 3 \cdot \log(x)$$

1.5 Simplify the following expression: $\log_{17}(x)$

Using the property of the logarithmic base change, the expression can be rewritten as:

$$\frac{\log_{10}(x)}{\log_{10}(17)} = \frac{\log(x)}{\log(17)}$$

1.6 Solve for x in the equation $\log_2(2^7) = x$

Using the definition of the logarithm:

$$2^x = 2^7$$
$$x = 7$$

1.7 Evaluate $\log_2(1) + \log_8(2^{120})$

Using the knowledge that $2^0 = 1$, $\log_2(1) = 0$. Rewriting the second logarithm as $\log_8(2^{3^{40}}) = \log_8(8^{40}) = 40$. Therefore the expression is equal to 40.

You can find practice problems for this chapter beginning on the next page.

Chapter 1 Practice Problems

Evaluate/Simplify the following expressions

1. $\log(3x) + \log(x)$

2. $\log(x^3) + \log(3xy)$

3. $\log(7x) + \log(3xy) - \log(3x)$

4. $\log(1000) - \log(10)$

5. $\log(x^3) + \log(x^{-3})$

6. $\log_2(2^7) + \log_3(9^2)$

7. $\log_2(4^{37})$

8. $\log_7(4) \cdot \log_4(7)$

9. $\log_x(y) - \log_y(x)$

10. $\log(z) - \log(3y) + \log(xyz)$

11. $\log_2(2^{\log_2(2^7)})$

12. $\log_x(1) + \log_y(y)$

13. $\log_3(27) + \log_2(8) + \log_{16}(2^8)$

14. $\log(2^4) + \log(5^4)$

15. $\log_2(3) \cdot \log_3(4) \cdot \log_4(5) \cdot \ldots \cdot \log_{98}(99) \cdot \log_{99} 100$

16. $2^{(3^{\log_7(49)})}$

17. $\log(2^3) - \log(2^2) + \log(2)$

18. $\log_3(6) + \log_4(8)$

19. $\log_e e^2 + \log_\pi \pi^3$

20. $\log(3xyz) + \log(4x^2y) + \log(7x^2y^2z^3)$

21. $\log(z^2) + \log(y^2) + \log(x^2)$, where $\log(x) + \log(y) + \log(z) = 8$

22. $\frac{1}{10} \cdot \log_3(1000)$

23. $2\log(x) + 3\log(y^2)$

24. $\ln(x^2) + \ln(e^4)$

25. $\ln\left(x^{\ln(e^{4x})}\right)$

26. $\ln(x) + \ln(x) - \ln(x^2)$

27. $\ln(\ln(e^e))$

Solve for x

28. $\log_x(7) = 3$

29. $\log_{(x^2+4)}(7) = 3$

30. $\log_8(x^2 + 16x + 128) = 2$

Chapter 1 Practice Problem Answers

1.a $\log(3x \cdot x) = \log(3x^2)$

2.a $\log(x^3 \cdot 3xy) = \log(3x^4y)$

3.a $\log\left(\frac{7x \cdot 3xy}{3x}\right) = \log(7xy)$

4.a $\log\left(\frac{1000}{10}\right) = \log(100) = 2$

5.a $\log(x^3 \cdot x^{-3}) = \log(1) = 0$

6.a $7 + \log_3(3^4) = 7 + 4 = 11$

7.a $\log_2\left(2^{2^{37}}\right) = \log_2(2^{74}) = 74$

8.a $\frac{\log(4)}{\log(7)} \cdot \frac{\log(7)}{\log(4)} = 1$

9.a $\frac{\log(y)}{\log(x)} - \frac{\log(x)}{\log(y)} = \frac{(\log(y))^2 - (\log(x))^2}{\log(x) \cdot \log(y)}$

10.a $\log\left(\frac{xyz^2}{3y}\right) = \log\left(\frac{xz^2}{3}\right)$

11.a $\log_2(2^7) = 7$

12.a 1

13.a $3 + 3 + \log_{16}(16^2) = 3 + 3 + 2 = 8$

14.a $4(\log(2) + \log(5)) = 4 \cdot \log(10) = 4$

15.a $\frac{\log(3)}{\log(2)} \cdot \frac{\log(4)}{\log(3)} \cdot \frac{\log(5)}{\log(4)} \cdot \; \cdots \; \cdot \frac{\log(99)}{\log(98)} \cdot \frac{\log(100)}{\log(99)} = \frac{\log(100)}{\log(2)} = \frac{2}{\log(2)}$

16.a $2^{(3^2)} = 2^9 = 512$

17.a $\log\left(\frac{8 \cdot 2}{4}\right) = \log(4)$

18.a $\dfrac{\log(6)}{\log(3)} + \dfrac{\log(8)}{\log(4)}$

19.a $2 + 3 = 5$

20.a $\log(84x^5y^4z^4)$

21.a
$2\log(z) + 2\log(y) + 2\log(x)$
$2(\log(x) + \log(y) + \log(z))$
$2(8) = 16$

22.a $\dfrac{1}{10} \cdot \dfrac{\log(1000)}{\log(3)} = \dfrac{3}{10 \cdot \log(3)}$

23.a $\log(x^2) + \log(y^6) = \log(x^2 y^6)$

24.a $2\ln(x) + 4$

25.a $\ln(x^{4x}) = 4x\ln(x)$

26.a 0

27.a 1

28.a $x^3 = 7, x = 7^{\frac{1}{3}}$

29.a $x = \sqrt{7^{\frac{1}{3}} - 4}$

30.a $x = -8$

Chapter 2: Limits
Basic Limits, Limit Properties, Limits of Infinity, Limits at
Infinity, and L'Hôpital's Rule

The Limit Concept

A limit is a tool used to find values that a function approaches. The formal mathematic definition is shown below, but you do not need to know it or be able to use it for the AP exam.

$$\lim_{x \to a} f(x) = L$$

If for every value $\varepsilon > 0$, there is a number $\delta > 0$ where

$$|f(x) - L| < \varepsilon \text{ and } 0 < |x - a| < \delta$$

This is very complicated mathematics, and it is not really necessary to understand the limit concept. The limit is simply identifying the value of a function as it gets infinitely close to the input value.

2.1 Let's try to identify the limit below using logic.

$$\lim_{x \to 1} x$$

If we put in x-values extremely close to 1 from the left, such as 0.99, then the function would equal 0.99. But what if we went even closer to 1? If we input 0.99999, then the function would equal 0.99999. If we continue to put in values closer to 1 from the left, we can see that the function continues to get closer to a value of 1. But how can we be sure that as x approaches 1, the function also approaches 1?

The limit is a mathematical way to get infinitely close to 1, without inputting the value $x = 1$. The limit of the function $f(x) = x$ as x approaches 1 from the left can be seen below.

$$\lim_{x \to 1^-} x = 1$$

However, a limit only exists if the same value is approached from the left and the right.

For a limit to exist, the limits must be equal from both the negative side and positive side of the value being approached. Mathematically it is written in the form below.

$$\lim_{x \to a^-} f(x) = \lim_{x \to a^+} f(x) = \lim_{x \to a} f(x) = L$$

However, if the limits from the negative and positive side of a value are not equal, then the limit does not exist.

$$\lim_{x \to a^-} f(x) \neq \lim_{x \to a^+} f(x)$$

$$\lim_{x \to a} f(x) = DNE$$

This means that for the limit of $f(x) = x$ as x approaches 1 to exist, the limit from the right also must equal 1, like the limit of the function from the left did.

If we input values extremely close to 1 from the right, such as 1.001, the function is equal to 1.001. If we go even closer, the function equals 1.0001 when $x = 1.0001$ and the function equals 1.000001 when $x = 1.000001$. As we get closer to $x = 1$ from the right, the function also gets closer to a value of 1.

This means that if we get infinitely close to 1 using a limit, the function will approach a value of 1.

$$\lim_{x \to 1^+} x = 1$$

This means that the limit of $f(x) = x$ as x approaches 1 is 1.

$$\lim_{x \to 1^-} x = \lim_{x \to 1^+} x = \lim_{x \to 1} x = 1$$

Let's look at a limit graphically.

2.2 On the following page is the function $f(x) = e^{-x}$ from $-1 \leq x \leq 1$.

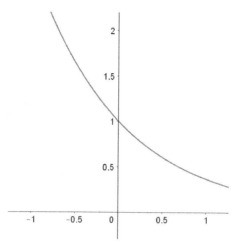

Let's identify the limit for the function as x approaches 0, given by the notation below.

$$\lim_{x \to 0} e^{-x}$$

Graphically, we can observe this using our function $f(x) = e^{-x}$

The limit of the function as x approaches 0 from the left.

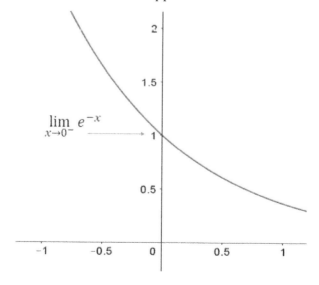

The limit of the function as x approaches 0 from the right.

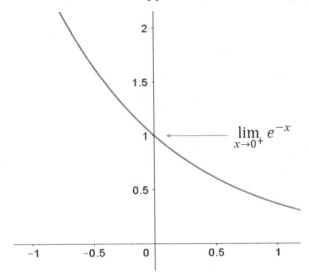

$$\lim_{x \to 0^+} e^{-x}$$

Since the limit from the right and the left are equal, the limit of the function exists.

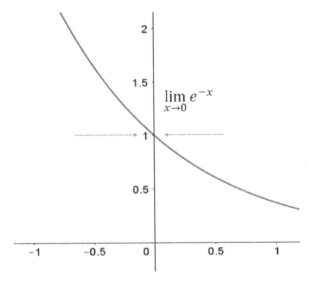

$$\lim_{x \to 0} e^{-x}$$

This makes sense, as when x-values infinitely close to 0 from the negative side and the positive side are input into the function, the function value becomes infinitely close to 1.

2.3 Let's observe the limit of the function $f(x) = \frac{x^2+3x+2}{x+1}$ as x approaches -1.

Algebraically, the function can be simplified to the form below.

$$f(x) = \frac{(x+2)(x+1)}{x+1} = (x+2)$$

This means that there is a removable discontinuity, or hole, at $x = -1$. That means that the function value at $x = -1$ does not exist.

$$f(-1) = DNE$$

Does that mean the limit does not exist?

If we input a value extremely close to -1 from the left, the function value is extremely close to 1. This means that the limit from the left exists in the form below.

$$\lim_{x \to 1^-} f(x) = 1$$

The limit from the right also exists, as value approaching the $x = -1$ bring the function value infinitely close to $f(x) = 1$.

$$\lim_{x \to -1^+} f(x) = 1$$

As the limits from the right and left exist, the limit then must exist.

$$\lim_{x \to -1} f(x) = 1$$

This means that limits can exist even if the output value does not exist. It is important to make the distinction that the limit of a function and the value of the function are very different.

One important technique for identifying limits is direct substitution, where the value being approached is directly plugged into the argument function. This is the method we have used thus far to identify limits. If a numerical value results and the function is continuous on the interval being observed, then the limit must exist at that value. However, this method does not always work, as we will see in later examples.

Basic Limits and Limit Properties

Limit Properties	
Constant (Where c is a constant)	$\lim_{x \to a} c = c$
Addition and Subtraction	$\lim_{x \to a}(a + b) = \lim_{x \to a} a \pm \lim_{x \to a} b$
Constant multiplication (Where c is a constant)	$\lim_{x \to a} c \cdot f(x) = c \cdot \lim_{x \to a} f(x)$
Multiplication	$\lim_{x \to a} f(x) \cdot g(x) =$ $\lim_{x \to a} f(x) \cdot \lim_{x \to a} g(x)$
Division (Where $\lim_{x \to a} g(x) \neq 0$)	$\lim_{x \to a} \dfrac{f(x)}{g(x)} = \dfrac{\lim_{x \to a} f(x)}{\lim_{x \to a} g(x)}$
Exponents	$\lim_{x \to a}(f(x)^n) = (\lim_{x \to a} f(x))^n$

2. 4 Identify the following limit.

$$\lim_{x \to 0} x + 2$$

Using the addition property, we can identify that the limit is of the form below.

$$\lim_{x \to 0} x + \lim_{x \to 0} 2 = 0 + 2 = 2$$

2. 5 Identify the following limit.

$$\lim_{x \to 2}(3x \cdot x^3)^2$$

This requires two limit properties: the multiplication and the exponent properties.

$$\left(\lim_{x \to 2} 3x \cdot \lim_{x \to 2} x^3\right)^2 = (6 \cdot 8)^2 = 48^2 = 2304$$

You may have recognized that the limit is also equal to the expression below.

$$\lim_{x \to 2}(3x^4)^2 = \lim_{x \to 2} 9x^8 = 2304$$

No matter which way you approach the problem, the limits are equal.

2.6 Identify the following limit.

$$\lim_{x \to \frac{\pi}{2}} \sin(2x)$$

Through direct substitution of the approaching value into the function, we can determine that the limit is of the form below.

$$\lim_{x \to \frac{\pi}{2}} \sin(2x) = 0$$

If direct substitution does not work, use one of the properties to simplify the argument of the limit.

Here are some trig limits that you should put to memory. These limits can be proved using L'Hôpital's rule, which is discussed later in this chapter.

Trig Limits	
$\lim_{\theta \to 0} \dfrac{\sin(\theta)}{\theta} = 1$	$\lim_{\theta \to 0} \dfrac{1 - \cos(\theta)}{\theta} = 0$

Limits of Infinity

2.7 Identify the following limit.

$$\lim_{x \to 0} \frac{1}{x^2}$$

Using direct substitution, $\frac{1}{0}$ results making the limit undefined and unidentifiable using this method. Let's observe the function graphically.

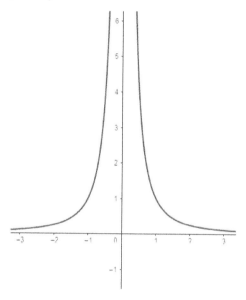

A vertical asymptote exists at $x = 0$, meaning that the function is undefined at $x = 0$. However, if we identify the limit from the left of $x = 0$, the function approaches infinity, and if we identify the limit from the right of $x = 0$, the function also approached infinity. This means the limit is of the form below.

$$\lim_{x \to 0} \frac{1}{x^2} = \infty$$

Technically a limit resulting in infinity does not exist, as the function at that value is quite literally limitless. However, infinity is often used to describe a limit rather than DNE as it is more descriptive of the function's nature.

Limits at Infinity

2.8 Identify the following limit.

$$\lim_{x \to \infty} e^{-x}$$

The value of x approaching infinity is not unlike it approaching any other value. If we use direct substitution, the limit results in the form below.

$$\lim_{x \to \infty} e^{-x} = \frac{1}{e^{\infty}} = \frac{1}{\infty} = 0$$

We can also identify this graphically.

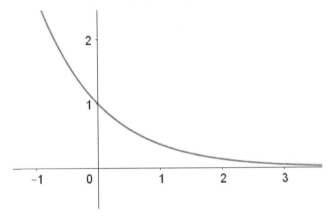

It can be seen that as x approaches infinity that the function continues to decrease towards $y = 0$. This is also the horizontal asymptote of the function.

Limits at infinity are often used to identify horizontal asymptotes and end behavior of functions.

2.8 Identify the following limit

$$\lim_{x \to \infty} \frac{3x^2 + 2x + 4}{4x^3 + 2}$$

When identifying the limit of infinity of a polynomial, identify the highest power polynomial present in the denominator and divide all the terms by the highest power term. In this case, the highest power in the denominator is in the $4x^3$ term. Then, after dividing, the limit is of the form below.

$$\lim_{x\to\infty} \frac{\dfrac{3x^2}{4x^3} + \dfrac{2x}{4x^3} + \dfrac{4}{4x^3}}{\dfrac{4x^3}{4x^3} + \dfrac{2}{4x^3}} = \lim_{x\to\infty} \frac{\dfrac{3}{4x} + \dfrac{1}{2x^2} + \dfrac{1}{x^3}}{1 + \dfrac{1}{2x^3}}$$

It is important to recognize that any limit of infinity of a polynomial with a constant over a function to any positive power is 0.

$$\lim_{x\to\infty} \frac{c}{x^n} = 0$$

Where c and n are positive constants.

Using this in the limit from the example, the limit can be simplified to form below.

$$\lim_{x\to\infty} \frac{0}{1} = 0$$

Notice how the denominator had a higher power polynomial than the numerator in this example.

2.9 Identify the following limit.

$$\lim_{x\to\infty} \frac{2x^3 + 2x}{3x^3 + 4}$$

After dividing by the highest power present in the denominator, $3x^3$, the limit simplifies to the form below.

$$\lim_{x\to\infty} \frac{2}{3} = \frac{2}{3}$$

Notice how the numerator and the denominator had equal power polynomials in this example.

2.10 Identify the following limit.

$$\lim_{x \to \infty} \frac{5x^6 + 2x}{4x^3 + 3x}$$

After dividing by the highest power term present in the denominator, $4x^3$, the limit simplifies to the form below.

$$\lim_{x \to \infty} \frac{\frac{5x^3}{4}}{1} = \frac{5}{4}(\infty)^3 = \infty$$

Notice how in this example, the numerator had a higher power polynomial than the denominator.

These three examples identify an important pattern for the end behavior of rational functions. The pattern can be seen in the table below.

End Behavior Patterns	
"Top Heavy" (Higher power exponent in numerator)	$\lim_{x \to \infty} \dfrac{ax^{n+1}}{bx^n} = \infty$
Equal Power Exponents	$\lim_{x \to \infty} \dfrac{ax^n}{bx^n} = \dfrac{a}{b}$
"Bottom Heavy" (Higher power exponent in denominator)	$\lim_{x \to \infty} \dfrac{ax^n}{bx^{n+1}} = 0$

Even though "top heavy" limits result in infinity, it does not mean they do not have asymptotes. The asymptotes for top heavy rational functions are usually oblique asymptotes, or angled asymptotes.

2. 11 Identify the limit and the oblique asymptote for the limit below.

$$\lim_{x \to \infty} \frac{3x^3 + 4x}{2x^2} = \infty$$

While the argument of the limit is a "top heavy" rational function and the limit is equal to infinity, the oblique asymptote must be identified through long division.

Through long division, the oblique asymptote of the rational function can be identified to be of the form below.

$$y = \frac{3}{2}x$$

This asymptote is graphed with the rational function below.

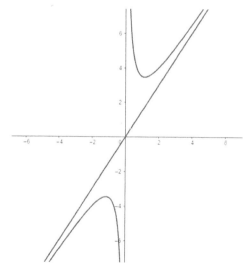

While recognizing the patterns for rational functions and their limits at infinity, it is still required that you prove their limit using the methods mentioned in this chapter.

L'Hôpital's Rule

What happens when a limit results in $\frac{0}{0}$ or $\frac{\infty}{\infty}$? These two forms are called indeterminate forms, where the limit or value cannot be determined from this result. In the table below are the various indeterminate forms you need to be able to recognize.

Indeterminate Forms	
$\frac{\infty}{\infty}$	$0 \cdot \infty$
$\frac{0}{0}$	0^0
1^∞	∞^0
$\infty - \infty$	$0 \cdot (-\infty)$

L'Hôpital's rule is a method for solving limits when either $\frac{0}{0}$ or $\frac{\infty}{\infty}$ results from direct substitution. However, the method only works for those two indeterminate forms.

L'Hôpital's rule uses derivation to identify limits. If you need a review of how to take derivatives, look at the derivatives chapter of this book.

The rule identifies that if either $\frac{0}{0}$ or $\frac{\infty}{\infty}$ result from direct substitution into a limit, that the limit is equal to the form below.

$$\lim_{x \to z} \frac{au}{bu} = \lim_{x \to z} \frac{\frac{d(au)}{du}}{\frac{d(bu)}{du}} = \lim_{x \to z} \frac{a}{b}$$

This merely states that you can take the derivative of the numerator and the denominator separately to determine the limit.

It is important to recognize that L'Hôpital's rule does not require the derivative of the entire argument of the limit, but rather, the derivative of the numerator and denominator of the argument separately. In other words, there is no quotient rule for L'Hôpital's Rule.

2.12 Identify the following limit.

$$\lim_{x \to 3} \frac{x^2 - 9}{x - 3}$$

Although this can be simplified using factoring, let's identify how the solution would result using L'Hôpital's rule. The form below results from direct substitution.

$$\lim_{x \to 3} \frac{x^2 - 9}{x - 3} = \frac{0}{0}$$

This step is critical for using L'Hôpital's rule. You must identify that the limit results in one of the two specified indeterminate forms to use the rule.

Now after taking the derivative of the numerator and the denominator, the limit is of the form below.

$$\lim_{x \to 3} \frac{2x}{1} = \lim_{x \to 3} 2x = 6$$

You will notice that the same result is achieved when solving the limit algebraically through factoring.

2.13 Identify the following limit

$$\lim_{x \to \infty} \frac{1}{x} \cdot e^x$$

Through direct substitution, we find that the limit is equal to $0 \cdot \infty$, which is one of the indeterminate forms, but it does not justify the use of L'Hôpital's rule. However, we can change the limit to the form below to justify use of the rule.

$$\lim_{x \to \infty} \frac{e^x}{x} = \frac{\infty}{\infty}$$

Now, after taking the derivative of the numerator and denominator, the limit is of the form below.

$$\lim_{x \to \infty} \frac{e^x}{x} = \lim_{x \to \infty} \frac{e^x}{1} = \infty$$

It is important to recognize that many of the indeterminate forms that do not justify the use of L'Hôpital's rule can be rearranged to then make use of this technique.

This technique will become very useful in later chapters.

L'Hôpital's rule is also used to compare the rate of change of different functions.

2.14 Identify which function is decreasing at a faster rate.

$$f(x) = -x^2, \quad x \geq 0$$

$$f(x) = -x^3, \quad x \geq 0$$

Using L'Hôpital's rule, we can put one function over another and identify the limit as x approaches infinity.

$$\lim_{x \to \infty} \frac{-x^2}{-x^3}$$

It is important not to simplify the argument, as the purpose of using L'Hôpital's rule in this instance is to compare the functions, not identify the overall limit.

Through direct substitution, we can justify the use of L'Hôpital's rule. The limit is then of the form below.

$$\lim_{x \to \infty} \frac{-2x}{-3x^2}$$

This still results in $\frac{\infty}{\infty}$, which justifies the use of L'Hôpital's rule a second time. There is no limit to the number of times you can use the rule, as long as it is justified by one of the two indeterminate forms.

$$\lim_{x \to \infty} \frac{-2}{-6x} = \frac{-2}{-\infty}$$

Now the limit does not result in $\frac{\infty}{\infty}$. However, the result helps us identify which function decreases faster. The numerator being a specific number, while the denominator is negative infinity then identifies that $-x^3$ decreases faster than $-x^2$ on the given domain.

2.15 Identify the following limit.

$$\lim_{x \to 0} \frac{1}{x} \cdot \tan(x)$$

As $\frac{1}{0}$ is undefined, direct substitution cannot be used to solve this limit. This limit also illustrates a very important concept about the existence of limits.

Even though the $\lim_{x \to 0} \frac{1}{x}$ does not exist, the limit in the example does in the form below. This limit is identified through the use of L'Hôpital's Rule.

$$\lim_{x \to 0} \frac{1}{x} \cdot \tan(x) = \lim_{x \to 0} \frac{\tan(x)}{x} \to \frac{0}{0}$$

$$\lim_{x \to 0} \frac{\sec^2(x)}{1} = 1$$

This means that even when one portion or all the parts of a limit do not exist individually, the limit as a whole can.

You can find practice problems for this chapter on the following page.

Chapter 2 Practice Problems

Identify the following limits using any technique.

1. $\lim\limits_{x \to 2} \dfrac{2x^3}{e^x}$

2. $\lim\limits_{x \to 2} \dfrac{x^3 - x^2 - 8x + 12}{x + 3}$

3. $\lim\limits_{x \to 0} \dfrac{\sin(3x + 1) + 1}{3x + 1}$

4. $\lim\limits_{x \to 0} \dfrac{x^3}{\ln(2x)}$

5. $\lim\limits_{x \to -1} \dfrac{x^2 + 4x + 7}{x + 1}$

6. $\lim\limits_{x \to 2} \dfrac{x + 2}{x - 2}$

7. $\lim\limits_{x \to \infty} \dfrac{2x}{4x^3 + e^x}$

8. $\lim\limits_{x \to 0} \dfrac{\ln(3x - 1)}{x^2}$

9. $\lim\limits_{x \to -\infty} \dfrac{e^{-x}}{3x}$

10. $\lim\limits_{x \to -2} \dfrac{\sin(2x)}{x + 2}$

11. $\lim\limits_{x \to \infty} \dfrac{(x + 3)}{x^3 + 2x}$

12. $\lim\limits_{x \to -4} \dfrac{x + 3}{x + 4}$

13. $\lim\limits_{x \to -4} \dfrac{1}{(x + 4)^2}$

14. $\lim\limits_{x \to -\infty} e^x + 4$

15. $\lim\limits_{x \to 1} \dfrac{x-1}{\ln(x)}$

16. $\lim\limits_{x \to 0} \dfrac{x^2}{|x|}$

17. $\lim\limits_{x \to 0} \dfrac{|x|}{x}$

18. $\lim\limits_{x \to 0} \dfrac{\cos(2x)}{x}$

19. $\lim\limits_{x \to -\infty} 2^x + 2$

20. $\lim\limits_{x \to 0} \dfrac{1}{|x|}$

Identify the limits of the following functions. If a discontinuity is present, identify the type of discontinuity.

21. $\lim\limits_{x \to 0} f(x)$

$$f(x) = \begin{cases} -x, & x < 0 \\ x+1, & x \geq 0 \end{cases}$$

22. $\lim\limits_{x \to 2} \dfrac{x^2 + x - 6}{x - 2}$

23. $\lim\limits_{x \to 3} f(x)$

$$f(x) = \begin{cases} -x^2 + 7, & x < 3 \\ x - 5, & x \geq 3 \end{cases}$$

Identify which function is increasing at a faster rate using limits.

24. $f(x) = x^2, \quad x \geq 0$

$f(x) = x, \quad x \geq 0$

25. $f(x) = 2^x$

$f(x) = e^{-x}$

26. $f(x) = \sin(x), \quad 0 \le x \le \dfrac{\sqrt{\pi}}{2}$

$f(x) = \sin(x^2), \quad 0 \le x \le \dfrac{\sqrt{\pi}}{2}$

27. $f(x) = x^3 - 2x$

$f(x) = x^2 - 2x$

28. $f(x) = x^3 - 3x, \quad 0 \le x < \infty$

$f(x) = x^3, \quad 0 \le x < \infty$

29. $f(x) = 4x$

$f(x) = 2x + 2$

30. $f(x) = 3x + 2, \quad x \ge 0$

$f(x) = x^2 - 3x, \quad x \ge 0$

Identify the following limits using any method.

31. $\lim\limits_{x \to 0} \dfrac{2x^2}{\ln(\sqrt{x})}$

32. $\lim\limits_{x \to 4} 2x^2 \cdot \ln(\sqrt{x})$

33. $\lim\limits_{x \to \infty} \dfrac{2x^2}{\ln(\sqrt{x})}$

34. $\lim\limits_{x \to -\infty} \dfrac{2x^2}{\ln(\sqrt{x})}$

35. $\lim\limits_{x \to 2} x - 2$

36. $\lim\limits_{x \to \infty} x - 2$

37. $\lim\limits_{x \to -9} \sqrt{x^2 - 82}$

Identify the following limits using the graph below.

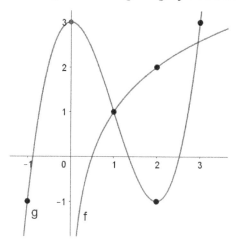

38. $\lim\limits_{x \to 2} f(x)$

39. $\lim\limits_{x \to 3} g(x)$

40. $\lim\limits_{x \to 1} f(g(x))$

41. $\lim\limits_{x \to -1} g(x)$

42. $\lim\limits_{x \to 2} \dfrac{f(x)}{g(x)}$

43. $\lim\limits_{x \to \infty} g(x)$

44. $\lim\limits_{x \to 0^-} f(x)$

45. $\lim\limits_{x \to 0^+} f(x)$

46. $\lim\limits_{x \to -1} \dfrac{g(x)}{f(x)}$

47. $\lim\limits_{x \to 3} f(g(x) - 2)$

48. $\lim\limits_{x \to 2} g(f(x) - 2)$

49. $\lim\limits_{x \to 0} f(x) \cdot g(x)$

50. $\lim\limits_{x \to 2} f(x) \cdot g(x)$

<u>Chapter 2 Practice Problem Answers</u>

1. $a \dfrac{16}{e^2}$

2. a 0

3. $a \sin(1) + 1$

4. a 0

5. a *DNE*

6. a *DNE*

7. a 0

8. a *DNE*

9. $a - \infty$

10. a *DNE*

11. a 0

12. a *DNE*

13. a *DNE*

14. a 4

15. a 1

16. a 0

17. a *DNE*

18. a *DNE*

19. a 2

20. $a \infty$

21. a *DNE*. Jump discontinuity

22. a 5. Removable discontinuity at $x = 2$

23. a -2

24. a $f(x) = x^2$ increases at a faster rate

25. a $f(x) = 2^x$ increases at a faster rate

26. a $f(x) = \sin(x^2)$ increases at a faster rate

27. a $f(x) = x^3 - 2x$ increases at a faster rate

28. a $f(x) = x^3$ increases at a faster rate

29. a $f(x) = 4x$ increases at a faster rate

30. a $f(x) = x^2 - 3x$ increases at a faster rate

31. a *DNE*

32. a $32 \ln(2)$

33. a ∞

34. a *DNE*

35. a 0

36. a ∞

37. a *DNE*

38. a 2

39. a 3

40. a 1

41. a -1

42. a -2

43. a ∞

44. a *DNE*

45. a $-\infty$

46. a *DNE*

47. a 1

48. a 3

49. a *DNE*

50. $a - 2$

Chapter 3: Derivatives Part I

The Limit Definition, Rules of Derivation, Basic Derivatives,
Trigonometric Functions, Inverse Trigonometric Functions,
and Derivatives of Logarithmic and Natural Functions

The Limit Definition

The derivative is an algebraic tool to determine the instantaneous rate of change of a function at a specific point. The derivative is also equal to the slope of the tangent line to a function at a specific point. The limit definition identifies how to determine the derivative of a function, $f(x)$, using the limit as Δh approaches 0. A derivative of a function is denoted by either $f'(x)$ or $\frac{d(f(x))}{dx}$, often seen as $\frac{dy}{dx}$.

$$f'(x) = \frac{d(f(x))}{dx} = \lim_{\Delta h \to 0} \frac{f(x + \Delta h) - f(x)}{\Delta h} = \lim_{x \to 0} \frac{f(x) - f(\Delta h)}{x - \Delta h}$$

The first form of the limit definition is the most common form seen and used throughout calculus.

Find $f'(x)$ for each of the following.

3.1 $f(x) = x^2$

After plugging the function into the limit definition, a problem can clearly be seen. The limit cannot be identified with Δh being 0, as it makes the limit undefined. Work must be done to try and simplify the expression so that the limit can be evaluated.

$$f'(x) = \lim_{\Delta h \to 0} \frac{(x + \Delta h)^2 - x^2}{\Delta h}$$

$$f'(x) = \lim_{\Delta h \to 0} \frac{x^2 + 2x\Delta h + \Delta h^2 - x^2}{\Delta h}$$

$$f'(x) = \lim_{\Delta h \to 0} \frac{2x\Delta h + \Delta h^2}{\Delta h}$$

$$f'(x) = \lim_{\Delta h \to 0} \frac{\Delta h(2x + \Delta h)}{\Delta h}$$

$$f'(x) = \lim_{\Delta h \to 0} 2x + \Delta h = 2x$$

The derivative of x^2 using the limit definition is $2x$.

3.2 $f(x) = \sqrt{x}$

After plugging in the function, the same problem arises as in problem 3.1. The conjugate of the numerator expression must be used to make the limit observable.

$$f'(x) = \lim_{\Delta h \to 0} \frac{\left(\sqrt{x + \Delta h} + \sqrt{x}\right)}{\Delta h}$$

$$f'(x) = \lim_{\Delta h \to 0} \frac{\left(\sqrt{x + \Delta h} - \sqrt{x}\right)}{\Delta h} \cdot \frac{\sqrt{x + \Delta h} + \sqrt{x}}{\sqrt{x + \Delta h} + \sqrt{x}}$$

$$f'(x) = \lim_{\Delta h \to 0} \frac{x + \Delta h - \sqrt{x} \cdot \sqrt{x + \Delta h} + \sqrt{x} \cdot \sqrt{x + \Delta h} - x}{\Delta h(\sqrt{x + \Delta h} + \sqrt{x})} \cdot$$

$$f'(x) = \lim_{\Delta h \to 0} \frac{\Delta h}{\Delta h(\sqrt{x + \Delta h} + \sqrt{x})}$$

$$f'(x) = \lim_{\Delta h \to 0} \frac{1}{(\sqrt{x + \Delta h} + \sqrt{x})}$$

$$f'(x) = \frac{1}{2\sqrt{x}}$$

Multiplying by conjugates is a tool that will likely appear on many problems when solving derivatives using the limit definition.

3.3 $f(x) = \cos(x)$

Be sure to remember trig identities for limit definition problems.

$$f'(x) = \lim_{\Delta h \to 0} \frac{\cos(x + \Delta h) - \cos(x)}{\Delta h}$$

$$f'(x) = \lim_{\Delta h \to 0} \frac{\cos(x)\cos(\Delta h) - \sin(x)\sin(\Delta h) - \cos(x)}{\Delta h}$$

Remember the cosine addition identity.

$$\cos(a + b) = \cos(a)\cos(b) - \sin(a)\sin(b)$$

Then recall that limits can be distributed across terms that are added or subtracted.

$$f'(x) = \lim_{\Delta h \to 0} \frac{\cos(x)\,(\cos(\Delta h) - 1)}{\Delta h} - \lim_{\Delta h \to 0} \frac{\sin(x)\sin(\Delta h)}{\Delta h}$$

It is necessary to recognize that the trigonometric functions of x can be factored out of the distributed limits, because they are not dependent on the limit. In other words, because the $\cos(x)$ and $\sin(x)$ are not in terms of Δh, they can be factored out of the limit.

$$f'(x) = \cos(x) \lim_{\Delta h \to 0} \frac{(\cos(\Delta h) - 1)}{\Delta h} - \sin(x) \lim_{\Delta h \to 0} \frac{\sin(\Delta h)}{\Delta h}$$

Finally, it is important to recognize two things that you should put to memory. These were shown in the limits chapter as well.

$$\lim_{\theta \to 0} \frac{\cos(\theta) - 1}{\theta} = 0 \qquad\qquad \lim_{\theta \to 0} \frac{\sin(\theta)}{\theta} = 1$$

Now, we can solve.

$$f'(x) = \cos(x)\,(0) - \sin(x)\,(1) = -\sin(x)$$

It is important to know that you may be asked to identify derivatives at specific points.

3.4 Identify $f'(\pi)$ if $f(x) = \cos(x)$. Use the limit definition to determine the derivative.

First, the function must be plugged into the limit definition and solved as seen above in problem 1.3. Then, once $f'(x)$ is solved for, π can be plugged in for the x-value in the derivative expression.

$$f'(\pi) = -\sin(\pi) = 0$$

Rules of Derivation

While the limit definition describes the exact mathematical process for determining a derivative, it is sometimes nearly impossible to solve. The following table identifies the set of rules used to find derivatives of functions.

Rules of Derivation	
$f(x) = c$	$f'(x) = 0$
$f(x) = ax$	$f'(x) = a$
$f(x) = x^n$ (power rule)	$f'(x) = n(x)^{n-1}$
$f(x) = g(x) \cdot h(x)$ (product rule)	$f'(x) = g(x) \cdot h'(x) + h(x) \cdot g'(x)$
$f(x) = \dfrac{g(x)}{h(x)}$ (quotient rule)	$f'(x) = \dfrac{h(x) \cdot g'(x) - g(x) \cdot h'(x)}{\left(h(x)\right)^2}$
$f(x) = g\big(h(x)\big)$ (chain rule)	$f'(x) = g'\big(h(x)\big) \cdot h'(x)$
$f(x) = \left(g(x)\right)^n$ (chain rule and power rule)	$f'(x) = n\big(g(x)\big)^{n-1} \cdot g'(x)$

Be sure to memorize these rules. Throughout the next few sections of this chapter we will explore how to use these rules in deriving simple functions.

Tips and tricks

Be sure to always put the $n - 1$ exponent when using power rule. It is easy to forget but is crucial to solving.

For quotient rule, the phrase "low d-high minus high d-low all over low low" may help in memorization.

Use whatever works best for you. It may be helpful to try and memorize the rules using words as well as in mathematic notation.

Basic Derivatives

Find $f'(x)$ for each of the following.

3.5 $f(x) = x$

The derivative of a variable of the first degree with respect to that same variable is always the coefficient of that variable.

$$f'(x) = 1$$

3.6 $f(x) = x + 1$

The derivative of a constant is always 0 so the derivative for problem 1.6 is the same as problem 3.5, since the coefficient for the variable in problem 3.5 is also 1.

3.7 $f(x) = 2x + 5$

The coefficient of the variable is 2, so the derivative is of the form below.

$$f'(x) = 2$$

3.8 $f(x) = 3x^2 + 7$

The presence of a second-degree variable makes it necessary to use power rule to find the derivative. (Technically power rule is also used for first-degree variables, but the variable portion just becomes equal to 1 as $x^0 = 1$)

$$f'(x) = 3(2)(x^{2-1}) = 6x$$

3.9 $f(x) = 9x^4 + 3x$

This problem also requires the power rule. Be sure to remember the exponent.

$$f'(x) = 9(4)(x^{4-1}) + 3(x^0) = 36x^3 + 3$$

3.10 $f(x) = 6x \cdot \sqrt{x}$

This problem requires power rule and product rule. Be careful when solving.

$$f'(x) = 6x\left(\frac{1}{2}(x)^{\frac{1}{2}-1}\right) + (\sqrt{x})(6) = 3x\left(x^{-\frac{1}{2}}\right) + 6\left(x^{\frac{1}{2}}\right)$$

$$f'(x) = 9x^{\frac{1}{2}}$$

You likely will notice that $f(x)$ can be simplified to $6x^{\frac{3}{2}}$ prior to taking the derivative. If you take the derivative from this point, you will still get the same answer.

3.11 $f(x) = \dfrac{7x^3}{(x+3)}$

Quotient rule is necessary to solve this problem.

$$f'(x) = \frac{(x+3)(21x^2) - (7x^3)(1)}{(x+3)^2}$$

$$f'(x) = \frac{21x^3 + 63x^2 - 7x^3}{(x+3)^2} = f'(x) = \frac{14x^3 + 63x^2}{x^2 + 6x + 9}$$

No further simplification can be done, so this is the final answer. You may notice that this problem can also be done using product rule when $f(x) = 7x^3(x+3)^{-1}$.

3.12 $f(x) = (9x + 2)^{-3}$

Chain rule and power rule must be used to derive this function.

$$f'(x) = (-3)(9x+2)^{-3-1}(9) = (-27)(9x+2)^{-4} = \frac{-27}{(9x+2)^4}$$

Be sure to remember all the parts of chain rule.

Chain rule will become more prevalent throughout the next sections.

Trig Functions

How do we take the derivative of a trigonometric function? First, there are some rules that you need to know.

Rules of Trigonometric Function Derivation	
Derivative of Sine	$\dfrac{d(\sin(u))}{dx} = \cos(u) \cdot \dfrac{du}{dx}$
Derivative of Cosine	$\dfrac{d(\cos(u))}{dx} = -\sin(u) \cdot \dfrac{du}{dx}$
Derivative of Tangent	$\dfrac{d(\tan(u))}{dx} = \sec^2(u) \cdot \dfrac{du}{dx}$
Derivative of Secant	$\dfrac{d(\sec(u))}{dx} = \sec(u)\tan(u) \cdot \dfrac{du}{dx}$
Derivative of Cotangent	$\dfrac{d(\cot(u))}{dx} = -\csc^2(u) \cdot \dfrac{du}{dx}$
Derivative of Cosecant	$\dfrac{d(\csc(u))}{dx} = -\cot(u)\csc(u) \cdot \dfrac{du}{dx}$

Chain rule and all other derivative rules still apply for trigonometric functions.

Find $f'(x)$ for each of the following.

3.13 $f(x) = \sin(3x)$

$$f'(x) = \cos(3x) \cdot (3) = 3\cos(3x)$$

3.14 $f(x) = 7\cos(3x) \cdot 2\sin(2x)$

All the rules of basic derivatives still apply to trig functions, making product rule necessary for this problem.

$$f'(x) = 7(-\sin(3x))(3)(2\sin(2x))$$
$$+ (7\cos(3x))(2\cos(2x)(2))$$

$$f'(x) = -42\sin(3x) \cdot (\sin(2x)) + 28\cos(3x) \cdot \cos(2x)$$

3.15 $f(x) = \cos^2(4x^2)$

Power rule and chain rule must be used to solve this problem.

It may be simpler to recognize how to derive this function when it is rewritten in the form below.

$$f(x) = (\cos(4x^2))^2$$

The necessity for power rule may be more clearly seen in this form.

$$f'(x) = 2(\cos(4x^2))^{2-1}(-\sin(4x^2)(8x))$$

$$f'(x) = -16x\cos(4x^2) \cdot \sin(4x^2)$$

It may help to replace certain parts of difficult functions with a different variable. For example, problem 3.15 can be done by replacing $\cos(4x^2)$ with u, where the function is now of the form below.

$$f(x) = u^2$$

$$f'(x) = 2(u)^1(u')$$

After replacing the variable u, we get the same answer.

$$f'(x) = 2(\cos(4x^2))(-\sin(4x^2)(8x))$$

$$f'(x) = -16x\cos(4x^2) \cdot \sin(4x^2)$$

Be careful with your derivation. Be sure to include all the parts.

Inverse Trig Functions

There are rules for deriving inverse trig functions just like there are for deriving traditional trig functions.

Rules for Inverse Trigonometric Functions	
Derivative of Inverse Sine	$\dfrac{d(\sin^{-1}(u))}{dx} = \dfrac{1}{\sqrt{1-u^2}} \cdot \dfrac{du}{dx}$
Derivative of Inverse Cosine	$\dfrac{d(\cos^{-1}(u))}{dx} = -\dfrac{1}{\sqrt{1-u^2}} \cdot \dfrac{du}{dx}$
Derivative of Inverse Tangent	$\dfrac{d(\tan^{-1}(u))}{dx} = \dfrac{1}{1+u^2} \cdot \dfrac{du}{dx}$
Derivative of Inverse Cotangent	$\dfrac{d(\cot^{-1}(u))}{dx} = -\dfrac{1}{1+u^2} \cdot \dfrac{du}{dx}$
Derivative of Inverse Secant	$\dfrac{d(\sec^{-1}(u))}{dx} = \dfrac{1}{|u|\sqrt{u^2-1}} \cdot \dfrac{du}{dx}$
Derivative of Inverse Cosecant	$\dfrac{d(\csc^{-1}(u))}{dx} = -\dfrac{1}{|u|\sqrt{u^2-1}} \cdot \dfrac{du}{dx}$

Notice the patterns between related functions, such as inverse tangent and inverse cotangent. Noticing the patterns may help in memorization.

3.16 $f(x) = \cos^{-1}(3x^2 + 6)$

Using the rule above, we find that the derivative is of the form below. Be sure to simplify the expression completely.

$$f'(x) = -\frac{1}{\sqrt{1-(3x^2+6)^2}} \cdot (6x) = \frac{-6x}{\sqrt{-9x^4 - 36x^2 - 35}}$$

3.17 $f(x) = \cot^{-1}(3x) + 2\csc^{-1}(x^3)$

Be sure to remember chain rule, as all regular derivative rules still apply when deriving inverse trig functions.

$$f'(x) = \frac{-3}{1 + (3x)^2} - \frac{2}{|x^3|\sqrt{x^6 - 1}} \cdot 3x^2$$

After simplifying, we arrive at the result below.

$$f'(x) = \frac{-3}{1 + 9x^2} - \frac{6}{x\sqrt{x^6 - 1}}$$

3.18 $f(x) = \sec^{-1}(\sin(x) + 6)$

This may seem difficult, but it can be done with careful work. Be careful with chain rule.

$$f'(x) = \frac{1}{|\sin(x) + 6|\sqrt{((\sin(x) + 6)^2) - 1}} \cdot \cos(x)$$

While this is a rather tedious example, it does identify the importance of recognizing the difference between an inverse trig function and a traditional trig function. Remember that their derivative rules are different.

After further simplifying, we arrive at the result below.

$$f'(x) = \frac{\cos(x)}{|\sin(x) + 6|\sqrt{((\sin(x) + 6)^2) - 1}}$$

You also may be asked to evaluate the slopes of tangent lines at specific points of derivations with inverse trig functions. Be careful when plugging in values.

Also recognize that an inverse trig function, such as $\sin^{-1}(x)$, can be rewritten as $\arcsin(x)$. This is true for all of the inverse trig functions.

Logarithmic and Natural Functions

One type of problem we haven't approached is functions with logs and exponential functions in terms of e.

Rules for Natural Functions	
$f(x) = \ln(u)$	$f'(x) = \dfrac{1}{u} \cdot \dfrac{du}{dx}$
$f(x) = \log_a(u) = \dfrac{\ln(u)}{\ln(a)}$	$f'(x) = \dfrac{1}{\ln(a)} \cdot \dfrac{1}{u} \cdot \dfrac{du}{dx}$
$f(x) = e^u$	$f'(x) = e^u \cdot \dfrac{du}{dx}$

It is important to remember that logs must be with base e to derive in this manner. You can use the change of base formula mentioned in the logarithmic functions if you run into a log not of base e. The method is shown in row 2 in the table above.

3.19 $f(x) = \ln(3x)$

The use of u replacements mentioned in the trig derivation section may be very useful for natural function derivation.

$$u = 3x$$

$$f(x) = \ln(u)$$

$$f'(x) = \frac{1}{u}(u') = \frac{1}{3x}(3) = \frac{1}{x}$$

This can be done without the use of u, but this tool may make more complicated problems easier in the future.

3. 20 $f(x) = \ln(3x) \cdot \ln(7x)^2$

It is also crucial to remember log properties when deriving logarithmic functions. Deriving coefficients is always easier than using power rule.

$$f(x) = \ln(3x) \cdot 2\ln(7x)$$

$$f'(x) = \ln(3x)\left(\frac{2}{7x}(7)\right) + (2\ln(7x))\left(\frac{1}{3x}(3)\right)$$

$$f'(x) = \frac{2\ln(3x)}{x} + \frac{2\ln(7x)}{x} = \frac{\ln(9x^2 \cdot 49x^2)}{x} = \frac{\ln(441x^4)}{x}$$

Log properties are also useful in simplifying the derivative.

3. 21 $f(x) = 7e^{3x+7}$

It may be useful to replace the exponent with a variable u. No matter how it is solved, the answer is of the form below.

$$f'(x) = 7\left(e^{3x+7}(3)\right) = 21e^{3x+7}$$

All rules of basic derivation apply to derivatives of natural functions. Be sure to use the rules when they apply.

3. 22 $f(x) = 10^x$

Unfortunately, basic derivative rules do not work for exponentials with a base other than e. The natural log can be used in exponential problems to make deriving simpler.

$$\ln(f(x)) = \ln(10)^x = x \cdot \ln(10)$$

Now $\ln(10)$ is just a constant, making deriving rather simple. However, it is important to recognize that you are no longer just deriving $f(x)$.

$$\frac{1}{f(x)} \cdot f'(x) = \ln(10)$$

It is important to isolate $f'(x)$ when using the natural log tool.

$$f'(x) = \ln(10) \cdot f(x) = \ln(10) \cdot 10^x$$

Be sure to replace $f(x)$ with the original function.

3.23 $f(x) = 4^x \cdot 5^{x+3}$

Once again, the natural log is needed.

$$\ln\big(f(x)\big) = \ln(4^x \cdot 5^{x+3}) = \ln(4^x) + \ln(5^{x+3})$$

Log properties make this derivative much simpler.

$$f(x) = x(\ln(4)) + (x+3)(\ln(5))$$

$$\frac{1}{f(x)} \cdot f'(x) = \ln(4) + \ln(5)$$

$$f'(x) = \ln(4) \cdot f(x) + \ln(5) \cdot f(x)$$

$$f'(x) = \ln(4)\,(4^x \cdot 5^{x+3}) + \ln(5)\,(4^x \cdot 5^{x+3})$$

It is necessary to replace $f(x)$ with the original function to find the final answer.

You can find practice problems over this chapter on the following page.

Chapter 3 Practice Problems

Using the limit definition, find $f'(x)$ for 1 and 2.

1. $f(x) = \dfrac{1}{x}$

2. $f(x) = \dfrac{1}{(x)^2}$

Find $f'(x)$ for each of the following.

3. $f(x) = \ln(2x + 7)^2$

4. $f(x) = (\ln(2x + 7))^2$

5. $f(x) = 4e^{\ln(2x)}$

6. $f(x) = 12x \cdot e^{4x} \cdot \csc(3x)$

7. $f(x) = 3x^2 \cdot \csc^2(4x)$

8. $f(x) = \dfrac{\tan(x)}{\ln(3x)}$

9. $f(x) = 7(x^2 + 2x^3)$

10. $f(x) = \ln(6x) \cdot x^3 \cdot \tan(x)$

11. $f(x) = \tan^2(2x)$

12. $f(x) = \sqrt{x} \cdot \cot(2x)$

13. $f(x) = \log(10x)$

14. $f(x) = e^x \cdot \ln(2x)$

15. $f(x) = x + \dfrac{1}{3x}$

16. $f(x) = \dfrac{1}{3x^2 \cdot \ln(x)}$

17. $f(x) = \dfrac{1}{x^2} + \sec(x) + x^3$

18. $f(x) = 4x^2 \cdot \arctan(x)$

19. $f(x) = x^2 e^{5x} + 3$

20. $f(x) = e^{5x^2} + 3$

21. $f(x) = 3^x$

22. $f(x) = 6x^3 + e^{\tan(2x)}$

23. $f(x) = \sin(2x) + 4\arcsin(2x)$

24. $f(x) = \ln(4x^3) \cdot e^{2x}$

25. $f(x) = e^{3x} - \text{arccsc}(2x)$

26. $f(x) = \log_3(\tan(2x))$

27. $f(x) = \log_2(e^x)$

28. $f(x) = e^{x^2} \cdot \sin(3x^2)$

29. $f(x) = \ln(e^4) \cdot x$

30. $f(x) = 3x^2 \cdot \text{arcsec}(3x)$

Evaluate the derivative at $x = 3$ for each of the following problems.

31. $f(x) = 4x^3 - 2x$

32. $f(x) = 2e^x \cdot \sin(\pi x)$

Find $f'(x)$ for each of the following. Leave in terms of the variable given. Always derive with respect to x.

33. $f(x) = \tan^2(3z)$

34. $f(x) = \ln(3z)$

35. $f(x) = \tan^{-1}(\ln(x^2))$

36. $f(x) = \arcsin(\arccos(x))$

37. $f(x) = \text{arcsec}(2x^3 + \sin(2x))$ Hint: Do not simplify.

38. $f(x) = \sin(\arcsin(2x))$

39. $f(x) = \sin(\arccos(2x))$

40. $f(x) = \arcsin^2(3x)$

41. $f(x) = \arctan^3(\ln(x))$

42. $f(x) = \arccos(\cos(x^2))$

43. $f(x) = \arccos(e^x \cdot \sin(x))$

44. $f(x) = e^{\sin(x)} \cdot \arctan(2x)$

45. $f(x) = \ln(\arctan(x)) + \sin(x)$

46. $f(x) = \arcsin^2(x + 4)$

47. $f(x) = \tan(\arctan(\sin(x)))$

48. $f(x) = \arcsin^2(x) + \arccos^2(x)$

49. $f(x) = \ln(\sin(e^x))$

50. $f(x) = \ln(\ln(\ln(x)))$

Chapter 3 Practice Problem Answers

1. a $f'(x) = \lim\limits_{\Delta h \to 0} -\dfrac{1}{x^2 + \Delta hx} = -\dfrac{1}{x^2}$

2. a $f'(x) = \lim\limits_{\Delta h \to 0} -\dfrac{\Delta h(2x + \Delta h)}{\Delta h(x^2(x^2 + 2\Delta hx + \Delta h^2))} = -\dfrac{2}{x^3}$

3. a $f'(x) = \dfrac{4}{2x + 7}$

4. a $f'(x) = \dfrac{4\ln(2x + 7)}{2x + 7}$

5. a $f'(x) = 8$

6. a $f'(x) = 48x\csc(3x)e^{4x} + 12\csc(3x)e^{4x}$
$\qquad\qquad - 36xe^{4x}(\csc(3x) \cdot \cot(3x))$

7. a $f'(x) = \csc^2(4x)(-24x^2\cot(4x) + 6x)$

8. a $f'(x) = \dfrac{\ln(3x)\sec^2(x) - \dfrac{\tan(x)}{x}}{(\ln(3x))^2}$

9. a $f'(x) = 14x + 42x^2$

10. a $f'(x) = x^3\ln(6x)\sec^2(x) + 3x^2\ln(6x)\tan(x)$
$\qquad\qquad + x^2\tan(x)$

11. a $f'(x) = 4\tan(2x) \cdot \sec^2(2x)$

12. a $f'(x) = \dfrac{\cot(2x)}{2\sqrt{x}} - 2\sqrt{x} \cdot \csc^2(2x)$

13. a $f'(x) = \dfrac{1}{x\ln(10)}$

14. a $f'(x) = e^x\ln(2x) + \dfrac{e^x}{x}$

15. a $f'(x) = 1 - \dfrac{1}{3x^2}$

16. $a\ f'(x) = -\dfrac{2\ln(x) + 1}{3x^3(\ln(x))^2}$

17. $a\ f'(x) = -\dfrac{2}{x^3} + \sec(x)\tan(x) + 3x^2$

18. $a\ f'(x) = 8x \cdot \arctan(x) + \dfrac{4x^2}{1 + x^2}$

19. $a\ f'(x) = xe^{5x}(5x + 2)$

20. $a\ f'(x) = 10xe^{5x^2}$

21. $a\ f'(x) = \ln(3) \cdot 3^x$

22. $a\ f'(x) = 18x^2 + 2e^{\tan(2x)} \cdot \sec^2(2x)$

23. $a\ f'(x) = 2\cos(2x) + \dfrac{8}{\sqrt{1 - 4x^2}}$

24. $a\ f'(x) = \dfrac{3e^{2x}}{x} + 2e^{2x}\ln(4x^3)$

25. $a\ f'(x) = 3e^{3x} + \dfrac{2}{|2x|\sqrt{4x^2 - 1}}$

26. $a\ f'(x) = \dfrac{2\sec^2(2x)}{\ln(3)\tan(2x)}$

27. $a\ f'(x) = \dfrac{1}{\ln(2)}$

28. $a\ f'(x) = 2xe^{x^2}(3\cos(3x^2) + \sin(3x^2))$

29. $a\ f'(x) = 4$

30. $a\ f'(x) = 6x \cdot \text{arcsec}(3x) + \dfrac{3x^2}{|x|\sqrt{9x^2 - 1}}$

31. $a\ f'(3) = 106$

32. $a\ f'(3) = -2\pi e^3$

33. a $f'(x) = 6\tan(3z)\sec^2(3z) \cdot \dfrac{dz}{dx}$

34. a $f'(x) = \dfrac{1}{z} \cdot \dfrac{dz}{dx}$

35. a $f'(x) = \dfrac{2}{x + x(\ln(x^2))^2}$

36. a $f'(x) = -\dfrac{1}{\sqrt{1 - (\cos^{-1}(x))^2}} \cdot \dfrac{1}{\sqrt{1 - x^2}}$

37. a $f'(x)$
$$= \dfrac{6x^2 + 2\cos(2x)}{|2x^3 + \sin(2x)|(\sqrt{4x^6 + 4x^3\sin(2x) + \cos^2(2x)})}$$

38. a $f'(x) = 2$

39. a $f'(x) = \dfrac{-4x}{\sqrt{1 - 4x^2}}$

40. a $f'(x) = \dfrac{6(\arcsin(3x))}{\sqrt{1 - 9x^2}}$

41. a $f'(x) = \dfrac{3\arctan^2(\ln(x))}{x + x(\ln(x))^2}$

42. a $f'(x) = 2x$

43. a $f'(x) = -\dfrac{e^x\cos(x) + e^x\sin(x)}{\sqrt{1 - (e^x\sin(x))^2}}$

44. a $f'(x) = e^{\sin(x)}\dfrac{2}{1 + 4x^2} + \cos(x)\,e^{\sin(x)}\arctan(2x)$

45. a $f'(x) = \dfrac{1}{(1 + x^2)\arctan(x)} + \cos(x)$

46. a $f'(x) = \dfrac{2\arcsin(x + 4)}{\sqrt{-x^2 - 8x - 15}}$

47. a $f'(x) = \cos(x)$

48. a $f'(x) = \dfrac{2\arcsin(x)}{\sqrt{1-x^2}} - \dfrac{2\arccos(x)}{\sqrt{1-x^2}}$

49. a $f'(x) = \dfrac{\cos(e^x) \cdot e^x}{\sin(e^x)} = e^x \cot(e^x)$

50. a $f'(x) = \dfrac{1}{x \cdot \ln(\ln(x)) \cdot \ln(x)}$

Chapter 4: Derivatives Part II

Differentiability, Implicit Differentiation, First Derivative Test, Higher Order Derivatives, Tangent Lines, Euler's Method, Derivative Theorems, and Inverses

Differentiability

One thing that has not been considered when taking derivatives is whether a function is even differentiable, or able to be derived. To be differentiable, a function must be continuous and smooth on its domain.

For example, the function $f(x) = |x|$ is not differentiable on its entire domain as it has a sharp bend or cusp at $x = 0$. Therefore, the function is not "smooth" at $x = 0$ and thereby not differentiable.

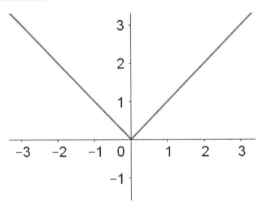

When a function is continuous, it means that the limit as x approaches a point from the right, from the left, and the value of x at that point are all the same value. This would be true for all values of x on a function that is continuous on its entire domain.

$$\lim_{x \to a^+} f(x) = \lim_{x \to a^-} f(x) = f(a)$$

If there is a point on the function that does not exist, meaning that there is a discontinuity on the function, there is also no derivative at that point.

It is important to remember that a limit can exist, even if the value at that point does not exist, but this does not justify continuity.

Implicit Differentiation

For all of the derivatives taken so far, the function being derived has been isolated for a single variable, usually of the form $y = f(x)$. However, there are some instances where an equation is not isolated in terms of a single variable.

4.1 $2y^2 + 2x^2 = 4$

This is where implicit techniques are necessary. If you recall, when taking a derivative of any variable, u, with respect to a variable, x, the derivative is equal to the expression below.

$$\frac{d(u)}{dx} = (1)\frac{du}{dx}$$

This is taken for granted while deriving equations isolated in terms of x because the derivative of x is $(1)\frac{dx}{dx}$ or 1. Implicit differentiation is simply an extra consideration of chain rule.

Let's apply this to the example. The derivative is taken in the normal way, just with the extra consideration for which variable is being derived.

$$2(2y)\left(\frac{dy}{dx}\right) + 2(2x)\left(\frac{dx}{dx}\right) = 0$$

This simplifies to the form below. You also may be asked to isolate for $\frac{dy}{dx}$.

$$\frac{dy}{dx} = \frac{-4x}{4y} = -\frac{x}{y}$$

For this example, we can leave it in this form.

4.2 $2y = 3x^3 + \cos(x)$ Find $\frac{dy}{dt}$

In this problem, we will not derive with respect to x but rather with respect to t. Implicit differentiation allows for the derivative to be taken with respect to any variable. This will become useful when solving velocity, optimization, and other problems in later chapters.

$$2\left(\frac{dy}{dt}\right) = 9x^2\left(\frac{dx}{dt}\right) - \sin(x) \cdot \frac{dx}{dt}$$

$$\frac{dy}{dt} = \left(\frac{9}{2}x^2 - \frac{\sin(x)}{2}\right)\left(\frac{dx}{dt}\right)$$

4.3 $y^2 = 4x^3 + 6z^2$ Find $\frac{dy}{dx}$

The introduction of the third variable should not be frightening. It is merely derived in the same way all the other variables are. Notice in the stem of the problem that we are asked to find the derivative of y with respect to x, which means we will derive with respect to x for all of the variables.

$$2y\left(\frac{dy}{dx}\right) = 12x^2\left(\frac{dx}{dx}\right) + 12z\left(\frac{dz}{dx}\right)$$

Now after isolating, we get the expression below.

$$\frac{dy}{dx} = \frac{6x^2}{y} + \frac{6z}{y}\left(\frac{dz}{dx}\right)$$

However, it is important to realize that you may be required to isolate the derivative in terms of x and z. That means the y variables present in the expression must be replaced.

From the initial problem, y can be isolated to the form below.

$$y = \pm\sqrt{4x^3 + 6z^2}$$

The final answer, then, is of the form below.

$$\frac{dy}{dx} = \pm\frac{\left(6x^2 + 6z\left(\frac{dz}{dx}\right)\right)}{\sqrt{4x^3 + 6z^2}}$$

Critical Points and the First Derivative Test

A critical point is where the derivative of a function is equal to 0. Critical points serve a very important purpose. They are also places where a function may have relative extrema. Extrema are either maximum or minimum values on the graph of a function. Extrema can either be relative or absolute. Look at the example below.

4. 4

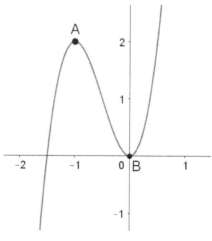

$$f(x) = 4x^3 + 6x^2$$

This graph has two relative extrema. It has a relative maximum at $x = -1$ and a relative minimum value at $x = 0$. This can be seen visually at the top and the bottom of the curved sections, marked by points A and B above. However, neither of these extrema are absolute extrema, because they are not the highest or lowest points on the function. The relative maximum value at $x = -1$ is not absolute, because the function tends towards infinity as x approaches infinity. This statement can be proven using a limit of the form below.

$$\lim_{x \to \infty} 4x^3 + 6x^2 = \infty$$

The maximum is considered relative, because it is the highest point on the graph in relation to the parts of the function around it. The maximum is higher or greater in value relative to all parts of the function on the domain $-\infty < x < 0.5$. The relative minimum value is considered relative because it is the lowest value of the function relative to nearby sections of the graph. The minimum at $x = 0$ is the lowest value of the function on the domain $-1.5 < x < \infty$. However, this extremum can also not be considered absolute, because the function tends towards negative infinity as x approaches negative infinity. This can also be proven using a limit.

$$\lim_{x \to -\infty} 4x^3 + 6x^2 = -\infty$$

While the extrema can easily be pointed out visually using the graph, this is not an accurate method for justifying that the highest point in that relative area is at that exact point. What can we use to prove the existence of extrema?

This brings us back to critical points. Where the derivative of a function is equal to 0, there exists a critical point, which is a potential place for the existence of a relative extrema. Let's look at the derivative graph for the function we observed before.

$$f'(x) = 12x^2 + 12x$$

The graph is shown below.

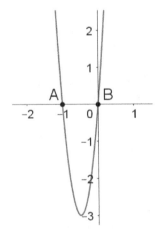

It can be seen that the graph is equal to 0 at the values $x = 0$ and $x = -1$, marked by point B and point A on the graph, respectively. However, the existence of a critical point does not guarantee the existence of extrema. For a relative max or min to exist at a critical point, the derivative function must cross the x-axis, changing either from positive values to negative values or negative values to positive values.

These are the principles of the first-derivative test, which identifies the existence of relative extrema.

First Derivative Test
If the first derivative changes from positive to negative across the value $x = a$, a critical point, then $f(a)$ is a relative maximum on the function $f(x)$.
If the first derivative changes from negative to positive across the value $x = b$, a critical point, then $f(b)$ is a relative minimum on the function $f(x)$.

Let's apply this test to the example function. On the graph of $f'(x)$, the derivative changes from positive values to negative values across critical point A, where $x = -1$. This proves that on the graph of the function, $f(x)$, there exists a relative maximum at $f(-1)$. The derivative changes from negative to positive across the critical point $x = 0$, proving that a relative minimum exists on the graph of the function at $f(0)$. This can be seen to be true looking back at the original function graph at the beginning of this section.

The first derivative test does not prove the existence of absolute extrema, as the relative extrema proved by the first derivative in the example function on the previous page are not absolute extrema.

To prove the existence of absolute extrema, it is necessary to first identify the function values at all the critical points, and then identify any horizontal asymptotes. In other words, it is necessary to test the end behavior of the function using limits at infinity, and then compare the value of the functions end behavior to the function values of critical points.

4.5 For example, let's examine the function $f(x) = x^2$

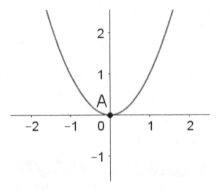

The vertex of the graph, point A, is a relative minimum where $x = 0$, which can be proven using the first derivative test. $f'(x)$ is shown below.

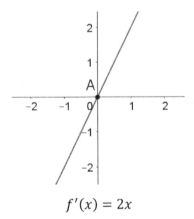

$$f'(x) = 2x$$

However, the vertex of the graph is also an absolute minimum, as the graph approaches positive infinity as x approaches positive and negative infinity, verified by using limits at infinity of the form below, and no other critical points or relative extrema exist.

$$\lim_{x \to -\infty} x^2 = \infty \qquad\qquad \lim_{x \to \infty} x^2 = \infty$$

Higher Order Derivatives

We have taken derivatives of functions throughout this book, but what if we take the derivative of a derivative? Taking a derivative of a derivative results in a second order derivative. Taking a derivative of the second order derivative results in the third order derivative and so on for n order derivatives. The derivation process is exactly the same no matter how many times you take the derivative. However, notation for higher order derivatives is a little different.

An n-th order derivative of the graph of y takes the form below.

$$\frac{d^n y}{dx^n} = y^{(n)}$$

Beyond the third order, derivatives using the prime symbol or the apostrophe, as seen in $f'(x)$, must be replaced with a number inside parentheses. For example, the first five derivatives of $f(x)$ are shown below.

$$f(x) = x^5$$

$$f'(x) = 5x^4$$

$$f''(x) = 20x^3$$

$$f'''(x) = 60x^2$$

$$f^{(4)}(x) = 120x$$

$$f^{(5)}(x) = 120$$

Notice how beyond $f'''(x)$ the prime symbol is replaced by a number.

It is important to check differentiability when taking higher order derivatives, as a function can be twice differentiable, but the third derivative at specific points may be unobservable, due to a cusp or sharp turn in the second derivative.

Concavity and the Second Derivative Test

While the first derivative shows critical points and relative extrema for a function, the second derivative shows concavity and points of inflection. Concavity refers to the shape of the graph. When a function is concave up, the graph appears in the shape of the letter "U," and when a function is concave down, the graph appears in the shape of an upside-down letter "U." For example, the function $f(x) = x^2$ is concave up on its entire interval, as the "U" shape is present.

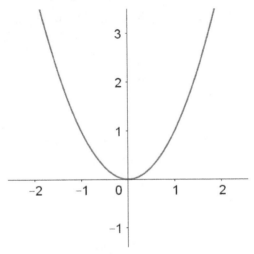

However, stating that the graph appears in shape of the letter "U" or an upside-down "U" is not enough justification to prove whether a graph is concave up or concave down. This is where the second derivative test comes in.

When the second derivative is equal to 0, there is a point of inflection on the graph of the function.

When the second derivative is positive on an interval, the function is concave up on that interval

When the second derivative is negative on an interval, the function is concave down on the interval.

Below are the graphs for $f'(x)$ and $f''(x)$.

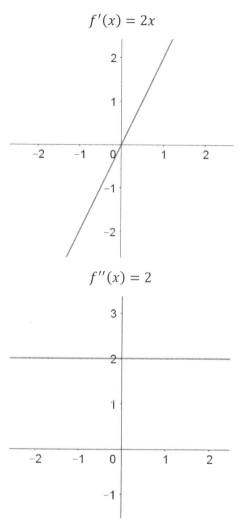

$$f'(x) = 2x$$

$$f''(x) = 2$$

The second derivative is positive on the interval $(-\infty, \infty)$, meaning that the function should be concave up on its entire domain. This can be seen to be true based on the graphs shown above.

According to the second derivative test, there are no points of inflection on the graph for $f(x)$, as there is no place where the second derivative is equal to 0.

A point of inflection is where the concavity of a function changes. This can be observed on the function below.

$$f(x) = 2x^3 + 3x^2$$

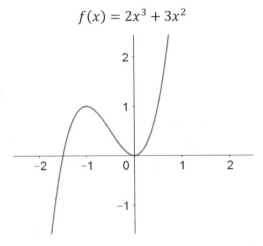

It can be observed visually that the graph changes from concave down to concave up somewhere between $x = -1$ and $x = 0$. This exact value can be found using the second derivative of the function and solving for the root.

$$f''(x) = 12x + 6$$

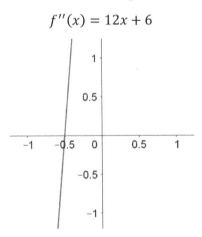

$f''(-0.5) = 0$, which means that the point of inflection for the graph of $f(x)$ is at $x = -0.5$.

Using Derivatives to Graph Tangent Lines

The basic formula used for graphing a tangent line is of the form below.

$$y - y_1 = f'(x_1)(x - x_1)$$

y_1 is the function value, x_1 is the corresponding x-value, and $f'(x_1)$ is the value of the derivative at the x-value. This is simply an adapted version of the point slope formula used for graphing linear functions.

4.6 $f(x) = x^3$. What is the formula for a line tangent to the graph at $x = 2$?

First take the derivative and plug in the x-value to find the slope of the tangent line. Remember, the value of a derivative is only the slope of the line tangent to the function at that specific point.

$$f'(x) = 3x^2$$

$$f'(2) = 3(4) = 12$$

We also need a y_1 value, as a point was not given. Simply plug in the x-value into the function.

$$f(2) = 8$$

The equation of the tangent line with all the parts is of the form below.

$$y - 8 = 12(x - 2)$$

This equation can be simplified to the form below, however this is usually not necessary to receive full marks.

$$y = 12x - 16$$

Euler's Method

Euler's method is a tool to approximate function values using the derivative of the function. The equation for the method is of the form below.

$$f(x) = f(x - h) + f'(x - h) \cdot h$$

h is the step size used in the approximation. You will be given a step size. It is important to recognize that the smaller in value the step size gets, the more accurate the approximation is. You may notice that this equation is very similar to the equation used for finding the equation of a tangent to a function at a specific point. Euler's method is simply an approximation using a tangent line.

4.7 $f(x) = x^2$ approximate the value for $f(1.25)$ using Euler's method and a step size of 0.05.

For Euler's method, we must start with an x-value value we know that is close to the x-value we are trying to approximate. For this example, we will use $x = 1$, where $f(1) = 1$.

x	$f'(x - h)$	$h \cdot f'(x - h)$	$f(x)$ $= f(x - h)$ $+ f'(x - h) \cdot h$
1	$2x$	$0.05(2x)$ $= 0.1x$	1
$1 + 0.05$	$2(1)$	0.1	$1 + 0.1 = 1.1$
$1.05 + 0.05$	$2(1.05)$	0.105	$1.1 + 0.105$ $= 1.205$
$1.10 + 0.05$	$2(1.10)$	0.110	$1.205 + 0.110$ $= 1.315$
$1.15 + 0.05$	$2(1.15)$	0.115	$1.315 + 0.115$ $= 1.430$
$1.20 + 0.05$	$2(1.20)$	0.120	$1.430 + 0.120$ $= 1.550$

First, add the step size to each consecutive x-value in the table. Then calculate the derivative for the x-value in the previous row in column 2 and multiply it by the step size in column 3.

Finally add the 3rd column to the value of the 4th column in the previous row together to get the $f(x)$ value.

Technically the first row and second column in the table are not necessary and should not be included when completing Euler's method problems. They have been included in this example to help clarify the method.

Let's compare the value that resulted from the method with the actual function value at $x = 1.25$.

$$f(x) = 1.5625 \approx 1.550$$

The approximation was an underapproximation as it was less than the actual function value.

This method should not be used unless specified by the question.

There are a few important tricks you should be aware of when using this method.

We can identify and predict the type of inaccuracy of the approximation based on the concavity of the function. For example, the function used in the example, $f(x) = x^2$, is concave up on its entire domain. This means that any approximation done using Euler's method will be an underapproximation, similar to the one that resulted in the example above.

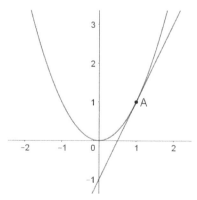

After observing the graph of the function and the tangent line to the graph at $x = 1$, which is marked by point A, it is clear that the approximation using the tangent line will be less than the actual function value, as the function increases at a greater rate than the tangent line.

If the function is concave down on the interval being approximated, the resulting approximation will be an over approximation by the same principle as above. When the function is concave down, it would be decreasing at a rate that is faster than the tangent line approximation.

Derivative Theorems

There are a few important theorems related to derivatives used throughout mathematics. These theorems are the Intermediate Value Theorem, the Mean Value Theorem, and Rolle's Theorem.

The Intermediate Value Theorem states, that if a function is continuous on an interval (a, b) and $f(a) \neq f(b)$, then there must be at least one value, c, where $a < c < b$ and $f(c)$ is between the values of $f(a)$ and $f(b)$.

4.8 For example, in the graph of $f(x) = x$ on the interval $(-1,1)$, $f(a) = f(-1) = -1$ and $f(b) - f(1) = 1$. The Intermediate Value Theorem identifies that there is at least one value of x, called c, where $f(c)$ is greater than -1 and less than 1. This is easily identifiable from the graph, where all the function values between the x-values of -1 and 1 are between the values of $f(-1)$ and $f(1)$.

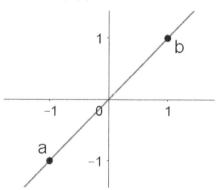

The Mean Value Theorem states if a function $f(x)$ is continuous on $[a, b]$ and differentiable on (a, b), then there must be a value c where $a < c < b$, so that the instantaneous rate of change or derivative at that value is equal to the average rate of change of the function on that interval.

In mathematical notation, this is identified by the equation below.

$$f'(c) = \frac{f(b) - f(a)}{b - a}$$

The average rate of change of a function on an interval is simply equal to the change in y divided by the change in x on the interval. This is commonly known as the slope of the line.

4.9 $f(x) = x^2$

$-2 \leq x \leq 1$

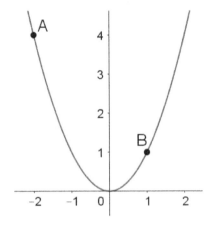

On the graph above, the average rate of change is shown by the expression below.

$$\frac{f(b) - f(a)}{b - a} = \frac{1 - 4}{1 - (-2)} = -\frac{3}{3} = -1$$

The Mean Value Theorem states that there is some value of x where the derivative of the function is equal to -1, as the function is continuous and differentiable on the interval.

$$f'(-0.5) = -1$$

The value c identified by the Mean Value Theorem is $x = -0.5$.

Rolle's Theorem is a specific application of the Mean Value Theorem.

Rolle's Theorem states that if a function $f(x)$ is continuous and differentiable on an interval (a, b) and $f(a) = f(b)$, then there is some value c where $a < c < b$ where the instantaneous rate of change at c is 0.

Using the same example, we can prove Rolle's theorem to be true due to the similar properties it has as the Mean Value Theorem.

4.10 $f(x) = x^2$

$-2 \leq x \leq 2$

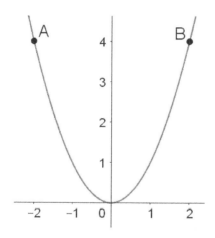

The average rate of change is equal to the expression below.

$$\frac{f(b) - f(a)}{b - a} = \frac{4 - 4}{2 - (-2)} = 0$$

As the average rate of change is 0 and $f(b) = f(a)$, there must be some value of x where the instantaneous rate of change is equal to 0 according to both the Mean Value Theorem and Rolle's Theorem. This value is $x = 0$ as $f'(0) = 0$.

Derivatives and Inverses

Recall from pre-calculus that the inverse of a function is the function's reflection across the line $y = x$.

4.11 Find the derivative of the inverse of the function below at $(7,1)$.

$$y = 3x^2 + 4$$

First, we must find the function's inverse. This is done by switching the placements of x and y.

$$x = 3(y^{-1})^2 + 4$$

$$y^{-1} = \pm \sqrt{\frac{(x - 4)}{3}}$$

The derivative of the inverse would then result in the form below.

$$y^{-1\prime} = \left(\frac{1}{6}\right)\left(\left|\frac{x - 4}{3}\right|\right)^{-\frac{1}{2}}$$

The value of the inverse's derivative at the point $(7,1)$ is then of the form below. Remember that the point on the inverse function is $(7,1)$, while the corresponding mirror point, or the point that is inverse to $(7,1)$, on the original function is $(1,7)$, as the values flip for a function's inverse.

$$\frac{1}{6\left(\frac{\sqrt{3}}{\sqrt{3}}\right)} = \frac{1}{6}$$

However, there is a simpler way to reach this derivative.

$$\frac{dy}{dx} f^{-1}(y) = \frac{1}{\frac{d(f(x))}{dx}}$$

This formula shows that the derivative of a function's inverse at the mirror point is equal to the reciprocal of the function's derivative at the original point. Looking at example 4.11 again, the derivative can be reached much more simply.

$$\frac{dy}{dx} = 6x$$

$$\frac{1}{\frac{dy}{dx}} = \frac{1}{6x}$$

Now, plug in the x-value of the coordinate on the original function, $(1,7)$, to get the form below.

$$\frac{1}{6} = \frac{d(y^{-1})}{dx}\bigg]_{x=7}$$

This was a much simpler method for determining the derivative of an inverse at a specific point. It is important to remember, that the reciprocal of a derivative of a function at point (a, b) is equal to the derivative of the function's inverse at the point (b, a). Do not get confused by the change in values.

Chapter 4 Practice Problems

For the following problems, determine if the function is differentiable on its entire domain. If so, graph the function of the derivative.

1. $f(x) = 3x^2$

2. $f(x) = \dfrac{1}{x^3}$

3. $f(x) = \ln(2x)$

Justify if the following functions are continuous at $x = 0$

4. $f(x) = x^3$

5. $f(x) = \dfrac{1}{x + 2}$

6. $f(x) = \ln(x^2)$

Find the next order derivative for each of the following.

7. $f'(x) = \dfrac{1}{x} + 6$

8. $f'''(x) = x^4 + x^3 + \cos(\ln(2x))$

9. $f''(x) = x \cdot \ln(2 \tan(x))$

Find the equation for the tangent line at $x = 2$ for each of the following functions.

10. $f(x) = 3x^2$

11. $f(x) = \ln(3x - 2)$

12. $f(x) = \dfrac{1}{x^3 + 4x + 6}$

13. $f(x) = \ln\left(\dfrac{1}{x^3}\right)$

14. $f(x) = \cos(x - 2) + \sin(x - 2)\csc(x - 3)$

Using Euler's Method, approximate the function value at $x = 2$, using a step value of 0.2, and starting with the value at $x = 1$. Also identify if your approximation is an under-approximation or an over-approximation and justify your answer.

15. $f(x) = 2^x$

16. $f(x) = \ln(3x - 2)$

17. $f(x) = \dfrac{1}{x^3 + 4x + 6}$

18. $f(x) = \ln\left(\dfrac{1}{x^3}\right)$

19. $f(x) = 3\cos(x - 1)$

Identify your percent error from the functions actual value for problems $15 - 19$.

For the following problems, identify and justify the existence of a value c where the derivative at $x = c$ is equal to the average rate of change of the function on the interval $-2 \le x \le 2$ using Mean Value Theorem and Rolle's Theorem when appropriate. Be sure to justify your answer appropriately using the theorems.

20. $f(x) = 3x^3$

21. $f(x) = 3\ln(2x + 5)$

22. $f(x) = e^{\sqrt{x}}$

23. $f(x) = 2x^4 - 2x^2$

For the following problems, identify any extrema and points of concavity and justify using the derivative tests. After identifying, draw the graph of the function on an appropriate domain and the graph of the second derivative for problems $24 - 25$.

24. $f'(x) = x^3$

25. $f'(x) = 3(x + 4)^4$

26. $f'(x) = \ln(x^2)$

27. $f'(x) = e^{-x}$

28. $f'(x) = 8x + 2$

29. $f'(x) = \sec^2(3x)$

30. $f'(x) = -\cos(2x)$

For the following problems find any existing relative extrema, a calculator may be used to find extrema. However, it is best if you can show the work by hand.

31. $f(x) = x^2 \cdot \ln(3x^2)$

32. $f(x) = 4x + 3x^4$

33. $f(x) = \tan(\ln(2x))$

34. $f(x) = e^{\log_{10}(2x)}$

For the following problems, identify the derivative and any discontinuities that exist on the derivative's graph.

35. $f(x) = e^{\cot(2x)}$

36. $f(x) = x \cdot \ln(x) - x$

37. $f(x) = 2^{3x}$

38. $f(x) = \tan(e^{3x})$

For the following problems, identify if the function is continuous at $x = -3$, and if so, identify the equation of the line tangent to the function at that point. You may leave the slope in terms of an expression if necessary.

39. $f(x) = \dfrac{3x}{10x^3}$

40. $f(x) = \dfrac{\ln(2)}{x^2 + x - 6}$

41. $f(x) = \dfrac{x+3}{\arcsin(x)}$

For the following problems, use implicit differentiation to find $\dfrac{dy}{dx}$. Do not worry about isolating y in terms of the other variables.

42. $y^3 \cdot \cos(y) = 4x^2 + \cos(x)$

43. $\dfrac{1}{y^2} = \arcsin(2y) + \sin(x^3)$

44. $\dfrac{1}{1 - z^2} = y^4 - y^3 - x^2$

45. $\ln(y) = 3^x$

Find the value of the derivative of the function's inverse at the points or values given.

46. $y = 5x, \quad y = 15$

47. $y = \sin(x), \quad x = \dfrac{\pi}{3}$

48. $y = \sqrt{x} + 2, \quad y = 4$

49. $y = \ln(x), \quad y = 1$

50. $y = e^{3x}, \quad (0,1)$

1. a $f'(x) = 6x$

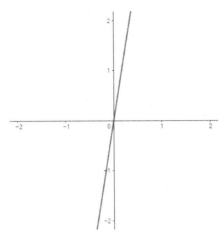

The function is continuous and has no cusps on its entire domain, making the function differentiable on its entire domain.

2. a $x \neq 0$, therefore, the function is not differentiable on its entire domain.

3. a $x \leq 0$ makes the function undefined, which means that the function is not differentiable on its entire domain.

4. a $\lim_{x \to 0^-} f(x) = f(0) = \lim_{x \to 0^+} f(x) = 0$. The function is continuous at $x = 0$.

5. a $\lim_{x \to 0^-} f(x) = f(0) = \lim_{x \to 0^+} f(x) = \frac{1}{2}$. The function is continuous at $x = 0$.

6. a $\lim_{x \to 0^-} f(x) \neq f(0) \neq \lim_{x \to 0^+} f(x)$. $\ln(0)$ does not exist, making this function discontinuous at $x = 0$.

7. a $f''(x) = -\dfrac{1}{x^2}$

8. a $f^{(4)}(x) = 4x^3 + 3x^2 - \dfrac{\sin(\ln(2x))}{x}$

9. a $f'''(x) = \ln(2\tan(x)) + \dfrac{x \cdot \sec^2(x)}{\tan(x)}$

10. a $y - 12 = 12(x - 2)$

11. a $y - \ln(4) = \dfrac{3}{4}(x - 2)$

12. a $y - \dfrac{1}{22} = -\dfrac{4}{121}(x - 2)$

13. a $y + \ln(8) = -\dfrac{3}{2}(x - 2)$

14. a $y - 1 = \csc(-1) \cdot (x - 2)$

15. a

x	$h \cdot f'(x - h)$	$f(x)$
1	-	2
1.2	0.277	2.277
1.4	0.318	2.595
1.6	0.366	2.961
1.8	0.420	3.382
2.0	0.483	3.865

This is an under-approximation because the function is concave up on the interval $1 \leq x \leq 2$, as $f''(2)$ results in a positive number.

15. b 3.375% (Using estimate from the table above)

16. a

x	$h \cdot f'(x - h)$	$f(x)$
1	-	0
1.2	0.6	0.6
1.4	0.375	0.975
1.6	0.273	1.248
1.8	0.214	1.462
2.0	0.176	1.639

This approximation is an over-approximation because the function is concave down on the interval, as $f''(2)$ results in a negative number.

16. b 18.229% (Using estimate from the table above)

17. a

x	$h \cdot f'(x - h)$	$f(x)$
1	-	$\dfrac{1}{11} = 0.091$
1.2	-0.012	0.079
1.4	-0.011	0.069
1.6	-0.010	0.059
1.8	-0.010	0.051
2.0	-0.00758	0.043

The approximation is an under-approximation because the function is concave up on the interval, as $f''(2)$ results in a positive number.

17. b 5.400% (Using estimate from the table above)

18. a

x	$h \cdot f'(x - h)$	$f(x)$
1	-	0
1.2	-0.6	-0.6
1.4	-0.5	-1.1
1.6	-0.429	-1.529
1.8	-0.375	-1.904
2.0	-0.333	-2.237

The approximation is an under-approximation because the function is concave up on the interval, as $f''(2)$ results in a positive number.

18. b 7.577% (Using estimate from the table above)

19. *a*

x	$h \cdot f'(x-h)$	$f(x)$
1	-	3
1.2	0	3
1.4	−0.119	2.881
1.6	−0.234	2.647
1.8	−0.339	2.308
2.0	−0.430	1.878

The approximation is an over-approximation because the function is concave down on the interval, as $f''(2)$ results in a negative number.

19. *b* 15.861% (Using estimate from the table above)

20. *a* As $f(x)$ is continuous and differentiable on the interval $-2 \leq x \leq 2$, $f(-2) = -24$, $f(2) = 24$, and the average rate of change is equal to 12, there must be a value c where $f'(c) = 12$ according to Mean Value Theorem. $c = \pm\frac{\sqrt{12}}{3}$.

21. *a* As $f(x)$ is continuous and differentiable on the interval $-2 \leq x \leq 2$, $(-2) = 0$ $f(2) = 6.592$, and the average rate of change is equal to 1.648, there must be a value c where $f'(c) = 1.648$ according to Mean Value Theorem. $c = -0.6795$.

22. *a* $f(x)$ is not continuous or differentiable on the interval $-2 \leq x \leq 2$, so Mean Value Theorems cannot be applied.

23. *a* As $f(x)$ is continuous and differentiable on the interval $-2 \leq x \leq 2$, $f(-2) = 24 = f(2)$, and the average rate of change is equal to 0, there must be a value c where $f'(c) = 0$ according to Rolle's Theorem. $c = 0$ and $c = -\frac{1}{2}$.

24. *a* Relative minimum exists at $x = 0$ as $f'(x)$ changes from negative to positive about $x = 0$. Point of inflection at $x = 0$, as $f''(0) = 0$.

$f(x)$

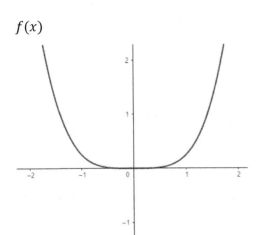

$f''(x)$

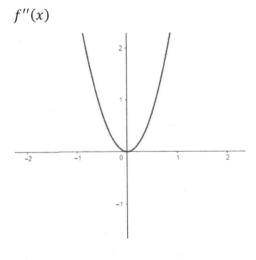

25. a No relative extrema as $f'(x)$ does not change signs. Point of inflection at $x = -4$, as $f''(-4) = 0$

$f(x)$

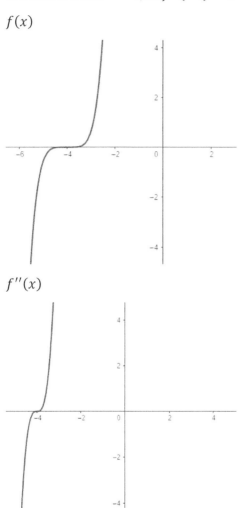

$f''(x)$

26. a Relative minimum at $x = 1$ as $f'(x)$ changes from negative to positive about $x = 1$. Relative maximum at $x = -1$ as $f'(x)$ changes from positive to negative about $x = -1$. No points of inflection as $f''(x)$ never equals 0. $x \neq 0$ for $f''(x)$.

27. *a* No relative extrema as $f'(x)$ never equals 0. No points of inflection as $f''(x)$ never equals 0.

28. *a* Relative minimum at $x = -4$ because $f'(x)$ changes from negative to positive across $x = -4$. No points of inflection as $f''(x)$ never equals 0.

29. *a* No relative extrema as $f'(x)$ never equals 0. $x \neq \frac{\pi}{6} + \frac{\pi}{3}k$ for all derivatives and the function, where k is any integer value. Points of inflection at $x = \frac{\pi}{3}k$, where k is any integer value.

30. *a* Relative minima at $x = \frac{\pi}{4} + \pi k$ as $f'(x)$ changes from negative to positive values at those x-values. Relative maxima at $x = \frac{3\pi}{4} + \pi k$ as $f'(x)$ changes from positive to negative at those x-values. Points of inflection at $x = \frac{\pi}{4} + \frac{\pi}{2}k$, as $f''(x) = 0$ at those x-values, where k is any integer.

31. *a* $f'(x) = 2x + 2x \cdot \ln(3x^2)$. Relative maximum at $x = 0$ as $f'(x)$ changes from positive to negative about that x-value. Relative minima at $x = \pm\frac{1}{3e}$, as $f'(x)$ changes from negative to positive about those x-values.

32. *a* $f'(x) = 4 + 12x^3$. Relative minima at $x = \left(-\frac{1}{3}\right)^{\frac{1}{3}}$, as $f'(x)$ changes from negative to positive about that value.

33. *a* $f'(x) = \frac{\sec^2(\ln(2x))}{x}$, no relative extrema exist. $x \neq 0$ and $x \neq \frac{1}{2}e^{\frac{\pi}{2}+\pi k}$ for the derivative, where k is an integer.

34. *a* $f'(x) = \frac{e^{\log(2x)}}{\ln(10)\cdot x}$. No relative extrema exist.

35. *a* $f'(x) = -2e^{\cot(2x)}\csc^2(2x)$. $x \neq \frac{\pi}{4} + \frac{\pi}{2}k$, where k is an integer value.

36. *a* $f'(x) = \ln(x)$. $x > 0$.

37. *a* $f'(x) = 3\ln(2) \cdot 2^{3x}$. No discontinuities.

38. *a* $f'(x) = 3e^{3x} \sec^2(e^{3x})$. $x \neq \frac{1}{3}\ln\left(\frac{\pi}{2} + \pi k\right)$.

39. *a* $\lim_{x\to -3^-} f(x) = \lim_{x\to -3^+} f(x) = f(-3) = \frac{1}{90}$, therefore, the function is continuous at $x = -3$.

Tangent Line: $y - \frac{1}{30} = \frac{1}{45}(x + 3)$

40. *a* $\lim_{x\to -3^-} f(x) \neq \lim_{x\to -3^+} f(x)$. $x = -3$ is a vertical asymptote.

41. *a* arcsine function's domain is restricted from $-1 \leq x \leq 1$ as graphing further would result in a failure of the vertical line test.

42. *a* $\dfrac{dy}{dx} = \dfrac{8x - \sin(x)}{3y^2 \cos(y) - y^3 \sin(y)}$

43. *a* $\dfrac{dy}{dx} = \dfrac{-3x^2 \cos(x^3)}{\dfrac{2}{\sqrt{1 - 4y^2}} + \dfrac{2}{y^3}}$

44. *a* $\dfrac{dy}{dx} = \left(\dfrac{2z}{(1 - z^2)^2} \cdot \dfrac{dz}{dx} + 2x\right)(4y^3 - 3y^2)^{-1}$

45. *a* $\dfrac{dy}{dx} = y \cdot \ln(y) \cdot \ln(3) = \ln(3)\,(e^{3^x} \cdot 3^x)$

46. *a* $\dfrac{1}{5}$

47. *a* 2

48. *a* 4

49. *a* 0

50. *a* $\dfrac{1}{3}$

Chapter 5: Integrals Part I

The Antiderivative, Properties of Integrals, Basic
Antiderivatives, u-substitution, Riemann Sums, First
Fundamental Theorem, and Average Value of a Function

The Antiderivative

An antiderivative, also known as an integral, is simply the operation that is the opposite of taking the derivative of a function. The integral of a function $f(x)$ is denoted by $\int f(x)dx$. The integral is an important tool in calculus, as it allows us to determine the area underneath a given function.

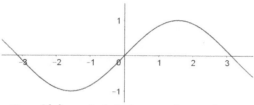

For the function $f(x) = \sin(x)$ shown above, the area under the curve is denoted by the shaded region on the interval $[-\pi, \pi]$. The areas shaded above the x-axis are positive values, and the areas shaded below the x-axis are negative values. In this case, $f(x) = \sin(x)$ is an odd function, so the shaded area under the curve equals 0.

When taking the indefinite integral of a function, a constant of integration must be included in the final answer, as the derivative of $x^2 + 3$ and the derivative of $x^2 + 7$ are both equal to $2x$. The constant of integration is usually included using the letter "C".

Thus the integral of the function $\int f(x)dx = F(x) + C$. The capital F is commonly used in calculus to denote the antiderivative of a function.

Properties of Integrals

Similar to the power rule for derivatives, the power rule for antiderivatives is stated as follows.

$$\int x^n dx = \frac{x^{n+1}}{n+1} + C$$

5.1 Evaluate $\int x^3 dx$

Using the power rule of antiderivatives, we obtain the following.

$$\int x^3 dx = \frac{x^{3+1}}{3+1} + C = \frac{x^4}{4} + C$$

5.2 Evaluate $\int x^{75} dx$

Using the power rule of antiderivatives, we obtain the following.

$$\int x^{75} dx = \frac{x^{75+1}}{75+1} + C = \frac{x^{76}}{76} + C$$

5.3 Evaluate $\int x^{5/4} dx$

Again, using the power rule of antiderivatives, we obtain the following.

$$\int x^{\frac{5}{4}} dx = \frac{x^{\frac{5}{4}+1}}{\frac{5}{4}+1} + C = \frac{x^{\frac{9}{4}}}{\frac{9}{4}} + C = \frac{4}{9}x^{\frac{9}{4}} + C$$

In order to make integrals easier to solve, we can manipulate the numbers and functions inside of the argument for simpler calculus. A basic property of integrals is denoted by the form shown on the next page.

$$\int kx \, dx = k \cdot \int x \, dx$$

Another basic property is the separation of two different functions in one integral into two separate integrals.

$$\int [f(x) \pm g(x)] dx = \int f(x) dx \pm \int g(x) \, dx$$

5.4 Evaluate $\int 6x^2 dx$

Using the properties of an integral, we can move the constant out of the integral.

$$6 \cdot \int x^2 \, dx = 6 \cdot \frac{1}{3} x^3 + C = 2x^3 + C$$

5.5 Evaluate $\int (3x^2 + 4x + 2) dx$

We can split this integral into three smaller integrals as follows using the additive property of integrals.

$$3 \cdot \int x^2 dx + 4 \cdot \int x \, dx + \int 2 \, dx$$

Using the power rule of antiderivatives repeatedly, we get the following answer.

$$x^3 + 2x^2 + 2x + C$$

Common Integrals

The antiderivatives listed below are commonly used throughout calculus. Refer to the chart below while performing integrations.

Basic Antiderivatives	
$\int k\,dx$	$kx + C$
$\int x^n\,dx$	$\dfrac{x^{n+1}}{n+1} + C$
$\int \dfrac{1}{x}\,dx$	$\ln|x| + C$
$\int \ln(x)\,dx$	$x\ln(x) - x + C$
$\int e^x\,dx$	$e^x + C$
$\int \cos(x)\,dx$	$\sin(x) + C$
$\int \sin(x)\,dx$	$-\cos(x) + C$
$\int \sec^2(x)\,dx$	$\tan(x) + C$
$\int \sec(x)\tan(x)\,dx$	$\sec(x) + C$
$\int \csc(x)\cot(x)\,dx$	$-\csc(x) + C$
$\int \csc^2(x)\,dx$	$-\cot(x) + C$

$\int \tan(x)dx$	$-\ln|\cos(x)| + C$
$\int \cot(x)dx$	$\ln|\sin(x)| + C$
$\int \sec(x)\,dx$	$\ln|\sec(x) + \tan(x)| + C$
$\int \dfrac{1}{a^2 + u^2}\,du$	$\dfrac{1}{a}\arctan\left(\dfrac{u}{a}\right) + C$
$\int \dfrac{1}{\sqrt{a^2 - u^2}}\,du$	$\arcsin\left(\dfrac{u}{a}\right) + C$
$\int \dfrac{1}{|u|\sqrt{u^2 - a^2}}\,du$	$\dfrac{1}{a}\text{arcsec}\dfrac{|u|}{a} + C$

u-substitution

u-substitution is a method for simplifying an integral due to the lack of a product or quotient rule of integration. In order to find the antiderivative of a more complex function, we must set the inner function equal to an arbitrary variable and then solve the integral. The u-substitution rule is defined by the formula below.

$$\int [f(g(x)) \cdot g'(x)]dx = \int f(u)du$$

In order to solve an integral using the u-substitution method, begin by setting the inner function equal to u, then take the derivative of u, and finally perform a substitution to solve the integral. The bounds of the integral may be substituted in terms of u, but this step is not necessary and will not be shown in the example problems.

5.6 Evaluate $\int e^{10x} dx$

Begin by setting the exponent equal to u.

$$u = 10x$$

Take the derivative of u with respect to x.

$$\frac{du}{dx} = 10$$

$$dx = \frac{1}{10} du$$

Perform a u-substitution using the formula provided.

$$\int \left[e^u \cdot \frac{1}{10} \right] du$$

$$\frac{1}{10} \int e^u \, du$$

Since the integral of $e^x = e^x$, we arrive at the form shown below.

$$\frac{1}{10} \cdot e^u + C$$

Finally, re-substitute the inner function for u, as shown in the form below.

$$\frac{1}{10} \cdot e^{10x} + C$$

5.7 Evaluate $\int (3x + 4)^2 \, dx$

Begin by setting the inner function equal to u, we can solve the integral more efficiently than by expanding.

$$u = 3x + 4$$

Take the derivative of u with respect to x.

$$\frac{du}{dx} = 3$$

$$dx = \frac{1}{3} \, du$$

Perform a u-substitution using the formula provided.

$$\int (u^2) \cdot \frac{1}{3} \, du$$

$$\frac{1}{3} \cdot \int u^2 \, du$$

Apply the power rule of antiderivatives to solve the integral.

$$\frac{1}{3} \cdot \frac{1}{3} \cdot u^3 + C = \frac{1}{9}u^3 + C$$

Finally, re-substitute the inner function for u.

$$\int (3x + 4)^2 dx = \frac{1}{9}(3x + 4)^3$$

5.8 Evaluate $\int 3x^2 \cdot \sin(x^3)\, dx$

Begin by setting the inner function equal to u.

$$u = x^3$$

Take the derivative of u in terms of x.

$$\frac{du}{dx} = 3x^2$$

$$dx = \frac{1}{3x^2}du$$

Perform a u-substitution by using the general formula provided.

$$\int \sin(u) \cdot 3x^2 \cdot \frac{1}{3x^2}du$$

$$\int \sin(u)\, du$$

$$-\cos(u) + C$$

Finally, re-substitute the inner function for u.

$$-\cos(x^3) + C$$

Riemann Sums

A common application of the integral is to calculate the area under the curve. In this case, a curve is any given function, and the area between this function and the x-axis can be calculated through the integrating operation. A Riemann sum estimates the area under a curve for a definite interval using the product of the output values of a function and a constant subinterval, as shown in the diagram below.

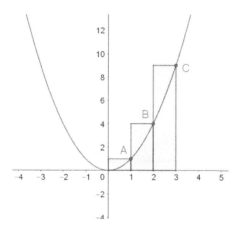

The Riemann sum shown above uses a fixed base interval and the function outputs to estimate the area under the curve of x^2 on the interval $[0,3]$.

The different methods of calculating the area under the curve using Riemann sums are described in the next section.

Types of Riemann Sums

Left Riemann Sums

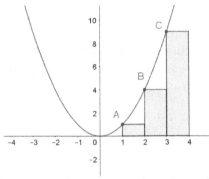

The method above uses the output values from the left-most value of the sub-interval on the x-axis. Notice that all the rectangles shown above are below the curve, and each have their top left corner touching the curve. This means that the left Riemann sum shown above is an underestimate of the actual area under the curve on the interval.

5.9 Use a left Riemann sum to estimate the area under the curve for $f(x) = x^3$ on the interval $[0,3]$ with $n = 3$.

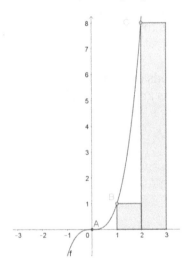

Drawing a quick sketch of the graph shows that the left output value on the interval [0,1] is equal to 0, the left output value on the interval [1,2] is equal to 1, and the left output value on the interval [2,3] is equal to 8. This means the left Riemann sum of x^3 on the interval [0,3] is equal to $0 + 1 + 8 = 9$.

Right Riemann Sums

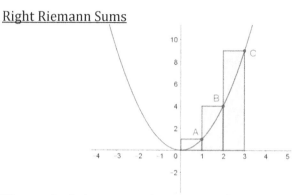

The method above uses the output values from the right-most value of the sub-interval on the x-axis. Notice that all the rectangles shown above are above the curve, and each have their top right corner touching the curve. This means that the left Riemann sum shown above is an overestimate of the actual area under the curve.

5.10 Use a right Riemann sum to estimate the area under the curve for $f(x) = x^3$ on the interval [0,3] with $n = 3$.

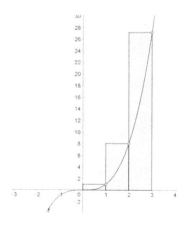

The diagram above shows that the right output value of the function on the interval $[0,1]$ is equal to 1, the right output value on the interval $[1,2]$ is equal to 8, and the right output value on the interval $[2,3]$ is equal to 27. Therefore the right Riemann sum is equal to $1 + 8 + 27 = 36$.

Midpoint Riemann Sums

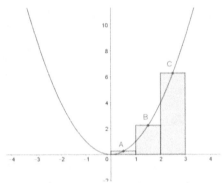

The method above uses the midpoint values of the sub-interval on the x-axis. Notice that all the rectangles shown above are partially above and below the curve. The sum of the areas of the rectangles shown above is seemingly close to the true value of the area under the curve. The midpoint Riemann sum provides a more accurate value of the area under the curve in comparison to left and right Riemann sums. This concept can be mathematically represented by the formula below.

$$\int_a^b f(x)dx = \Delta x[f(x_1) + f(x_2) + f(x_3) + \cdots + f(x_n)]$$

Where the function values are the outputs of the midpoint value of a given sub-interval, n is the number of sub-intervals, and $\Delta x = \frac{b-a}{n}$.

5.11 Use a midpoint sum to estimate the area under the curve for $f(x) = x^3$ on the interval $[0,3]$ with $n = 3$.

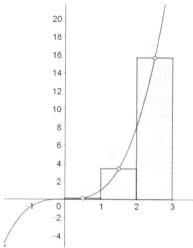

The diagram above shows the function outputs at the midpoint of each of the three intervals. The output value for the midpoint of $[0,1]$ is 0.125, since $0.5^3 = 0.125$. The output value for the midpoint of $[1,2]$ is 3.375, since $1.5^3 = 3.375$. The output value for the midpoint of $[2,3]$ is 15.625, since $2.5^3 = 15.625$. The sum of these three values is 0.125 + 3.375 + 15.625 = 19.125.

Trapezoidal Sums

The trapezoidal sum rule uses the formula of a regular trapezoid in order to estimate the true area under the curve. The formula for a trapezoidal sum is shown below.

$$\int_a^b f(x)dx = \frac{\Delta x}{2}[f(x_0) + 2f(x_1) + 2f(x_2) + \cdots + 2f(x_{n-1}) + f(x_n)]$$

Where n is the number of subintervals, and $\Delta x = \frac{b-a}{n}$.

5.12 Use the trapezoidal sum rule to determine the area under the curve of $f(x) = x^3$ on the interval $[0,3]$ using $n = 3$. Start by calculating the value of Δx.

$$\Delta x = \frac{3 - 0}{3} = 1$$

Next calculate function output values for the points being used in the trapezoidal formula.

$$f(x_0) = 0^3 = 0$$

$$f(x_1) = 1^3 = 1$$

$$f(x_2) = 2^3 = 8$$

$$f(x_3) = 3^3 = 27$$

Calculate the approximation using the formula provided.

$$\int_0^3 x^3 dx = \frac{1}{2}[0 + 2 \cdot 1 + 2 \cdot 8 + 27] = \frac{1}{2} \cdot [45] = 22.5$$

Simpson's Rule

Similar to the trapezoidal sum rule, Simpson's rule is given by the formula below.

$$\int_a^b f(x)dx = \frac{\Delta x}{3}[f(x_0) + 4f(x_1) + 2f(x_2) + \cdots + 2f(x_{n-2})$$
$$+ 4f(x_{n-1}) + f(x_n)]$$

5.13 Use Simpson's rule to determine the area under the curve of $f(x) = x^3$ on the interval $[0,3]$ using $n = 3$.

Start by calculating the value of Δx.

$$\Delta x = \frac{3 - 0}{3} = 1$$

Next, calculate function output values for the points being used in Simpson's formula.

$$f(x_0) = 0^3 = 0$$

$$f(x_1) = 1^3 = 1$$

$$f(x_2) = 2^3 = 8$$

$$f(x_3) = 3^3 = 27$$

Calculate the approximation using the formula provided.

$$\int_0^3 x^3 dx = \frac{1}{3}[0 + 4 \cdot 1 + 8 \cdot 4 + 27] = \frac{1}{3}[63] = 21.0$$

Definite Integrals and First Fundamental Theorem

The definite integral on the interval $[a, b]$ can be defined by the formula provided below.

$$\int_a^b f(x)\, dx = \lim_{\Delta x_i \to \infty} \sum_{i=1}^{n} f(x_i)\Delta x_i$$

Where x_i is the length of the sub-interval and $f(x_i)$ is the output value of the function.

In order to easily calculate the definite integral of a function, the First Fundamental Theorem of Calculus is necessary. The theorem is expressed in the form below.

$$\int_a^b f(x)\, dx = F(b) - F(a)$$

Where $F(x)$ is the antiderivative function of $f(x)$. Notice that the constant of integration is not required when applying the first fundamental theorem.

5.14 Calculate the area under the curve of $f(x) = x^3$ on the interval $[0,3]$ using the First Fundamental Theorem of Calculus

$$\int_0^3 x^3\, dx = \frac{1}{4}(3^4) - \frac{1}{4}(0^4)$$

$$\int_0^3 x^3\, dx = \frac{81}{4} = 20.5$$

5.15 Evaluate the following integral.

$$\int\limits_{0}^{10\pi} \cos(x)\sin(x)\,dx$$

Begin by solving for the indefinite integral using the double angle identity for $\sin(2x)$.

$$\frac{1}{2}\int 2\cos(x)\sin(x)\,dx = \frac{1}{2}\int \sin(2x)\,dx$$

Use a u-substitution to solve the indefinite integral.

$$u = 2x$$

$$\frac{du}{dx} = 2$$

$$dx = \frac{1}{2}du$$

Perform the u-substitution.

$$\frac{1}{2}\int \frac{1}{2}\sin(u)\,du$$

$$-\frac{1}{4}\cos(u) + C$$

$$\left[-\frac{1}{4}\cos(2x)\right]_{0}^{10\pi}$$

Apply the First Fundamental Theorem for the given bounds.

$$-\frac{1}{4}\cos(10\pi) - \left(-\frac{1}{4}\cos(0)\right)$$

$$-\frac{1}{4}(1) + \frac{1}{4}(1) = 0$$

Notice that the area under the curve is equal to 0. This is due to the fact that the function $f(x) = \sin(x)\cos(x)$ oscillates about the x-axis. The area below the x-axis is considered as a negative value, while the area above the x-axis is a positive value.

Average Value of a Function

The average value of a function on the interval $[a, b]$ is defined by the formula below.

$$\frac{1}{b-a}\int_{a}^{b} f(x)dx$$

The average value function provides a numerical method for evaluating the average output value for a function on a given interval. Half of the output values on the interval are above the average value, and half of the output values are below the average value. This method does not determine the average area under the curve but rather the average function value on the interval.

5.16 Calculate the average value of $f(x) = x^2 + 3x$ on the interval $[0,5]$.

Using the interval given in the problem, $a = 0$ and $b = 5$.

Substituting the intended values into the average value formula gives the form below.

$$\frac{1}{5-0}\int_{0}^{5} (x^2 + 3x)dx$$

This simplifies to the answer below.

$$\frac{1}{5}\left[\frac{1}{3}x^3 + \frac{3}{2}x^2\right]_{0}^{5}$$

$$\frac{1}{5}\cdot\left[\frac{1}{3}(5^3) + \frac{3}{2}(5^2) - \frac{1}{3}(0^3) - \frac{3}{2}(0^2)\right]$$

$$\frac{1}{5}\left[\frac{125}{3} + \frac{75}{2}\right] = \frac{95}{6}$$

You can find practice problems for this chapter beginning on the next page.

Chapter 5 Practice Problems

Evaluate the following

1. $\int (4x^7 + 5x^3 + 7x + 5)dx$

2. $\int (3x^2 + 5e^x + 10e^{2x})dx$

3. $\int 6x^2 \cos(x^3)\, dx$

4. $\int \dfrac{\ln(x)}{x}\, dx$

5. $\int (\tan(x) + \sec^2(x))dx$

6. $\int \left(\dfrac{5x}{9 + (x^2)^2}\right) dx$

7. $\int e^{x+4}\, dx$

8. $\int \dfrac{1}{x\sqrt{x^2 - 4}}\, dx$

9. $\int \sec^2(x)\tan(x)\, dx$

10. $\int 2xe^{x^2}\, dx$

11. $\int \left(\dfrac{-e^{-x}}{1 + e^{-x}}\right) dx$

12. $\int \dfrac{x}{3x^2 + 5}\, dx$

13. $\int \dfrac{e^{3x}}{9e^{3x} + 4} \, dx$

14. $\int \left(\dfrac{1}{15 + x^2} + e^{75x} \right) dx$

15. $\int x\sqrt{7x^2 + 5} \, dx$

16. Use a right Riemann sum with 4 sub-intervals to estimate

$$\int_0^4 (x^4 + 5) \, dx.$$

17. Use a right Riemann sum with 6 sub-intervals to estimate

$$\int_0^3 (x^3 + 2x^2 + 3x) \, dx.$$

18. Use a left Riemann sum with 3 sub-intervals to estimate

$$\int_0^{\frac{3\pi}{2}} \cos(x) \, dx.$$

19. Use a left Riemann sum with 3 sub-intervals to estimate

$$\int_1^4 (4x^4 + 3) \, dx.$$

20. Use a Midpoint Riemann sum with 2 sub-intervals to estimate

$$\int_0^4 (x^2 + 1) \, dx.$$

21. Use a Midpoint Riemann sum with 2 sub-intervals to estimate

$$\int_0^\pi (\cos(x) + \sin(x))\, dx.$$

22. Use the following table to calculate a right Riemann sum on the interval $[0,4]$, $(\Delta x = 1)$.

x	0	1	2	3	4
$f(x)$	5	7	1	6	8

23. Use the following table to calculate a right Riemann sum on the interval $[0,2]$, $(\Delta x = 0.5)$.

x	0	0.5	1	1.5	2.0
$f(x)$	4	8	5	3	7

24. Use the following table to calculate a left Riemann sum on the interval $[0,4]$, $(\Delta x = 1)$.

x	0	1	2	3	4
$f(x)$	4	8	5	3	7

25. Use the following table to calculate a left Riemann sum on the interval $[0,2]$, $(\Delta x = 0.5)$.

x	0	0.5	1	1.5	2.0
$f(x)$	4	6	5	3	7

26. Use the following table to calculate a midpoint Riemann sum on the interval $[0,6]$, $n = 3$.

x	0	1	2	3	4	5	6
$f(x)$	4	8	5	3	7	4	8

27. Use the following table to calculate a midpoint Riemann sum on the interval $[0,4]$, $n = 2$.

x	0	1	2	3	4
$f(x)$	1	3	2	4	8

28. Use a trapezoidal sum to approximate the area under the curve for the function $f(x) = 3x^2$ on the interval $[0,6]$ with $n = 6$.

29. Use a trapezoidal sum to approximate the area under the curve for the function $f(x) = x^5 - x^2$ on the interval $[0,4]$ with $n = 4$.

30. Use Simpson's rule to estimate the area under the curve for the function $f(x) = x^2 + 2x + 2$ on the interval $[0,3]$ with $n = 3$.

31. $\displaystyle\int_0^5 (3x^2 + 7x + 4)dx$

32. $\displaystyle\int_0^\pi 3\cos(3x)\, dx$

33. $\displaystyle\int_0^7 x^2 e^{x^3} dx$

34. $\displaystyle\int_1^2 \frac{\ln(x)}{x} dx$

35. $\displaystyle\int_{-3}^6 \cos(x) + \sin(x)\, dx$

36. $\displaystyle\int_{0}^{2\pi} \tan(x)\, dx$

37. $\displaystyle\int_{0}^{2} (3x^2 + e^x)\, dx$

38. $\displaystyle\int_{-10}^{10} (7x^9 + 3x^4 + 2x^2 + 5)\, dx$

39. $\displaystyle\int_{0}^{\pi} \sec(x)\tan(x)\, dx$

40. $\displaystyle\int_{-1}^{1} \frac{1}{1 + x^2}\, dx$

41. $\displaystyle\int_{-5}^{2} (e^x + 5)\, dx$

42. $\displaystyle\int_{1}^{e^2} \left(\frac{1}{x} + 2\right) dx$

43. $\displaystyle\int_{0}^{\frac{\pi}{2}} \sin(2x + \pi)\, dx$

44. $\displaystyle\int_{2}^{5} (x^2 e^2)\, dx$

45. $\displaystyle\int_{1}^{2}\left(e^{7x+5} + \frac{\ln(x)}{x}\right) dx$

For each of the following, calculate the average value of the function on the given intervals.

46. $f(x) = x^3 + 2x^2$, $[0,5]$

47. $f(x) = e^{2x} + 5$, $[0,3]$

48. $f(x) = \sin(x)\cos(x)$, $\left[0, \frac{\pi}{2}\right]$

49. $f(x) = \tan(x)$, $\left[0, \frac{\pi}{3}\right]$

50. $f(x) = 3x^2 + \sin(x)$, $[0, \pi]$

Chapter 5 Practice Problem Answers

1. $a \ \frac{1}{2}x^8 + \frac{5}{4}x^4 + \frac{7}{2}x^2 + 5x + C$

2. $a \ x^3 + 5e^x + 5e^{2x} + C$

3. $a \ 2\sin(x^3) + C$

4. $a \ \frac{1}{2}(\ln(x))^2 + C$

5. $a \ -\ln|\cos(x)| + \tan(x) + C$

6. $a \ \frac{5}{6}\arctan\left(\frac{x^2}{3}\right) + C$

7. $a \ e^{x+4} + C$

8. $a \ \frac{1}{2}\text{arcsec}\left(\frac{|x|}{2}\right) + C$

9. $a \ \frac{1}{2}\tan^2(x) + C$

10. $a \ e^{x^2} + C$

11. $a \ \ln|1 + e^{-x}| + C$

12. $a \ \frac{1}{6}\ln|3x^2 + 5| + C$

13. $a \ \frac{1}{27}\ln|9e^{3x} + 4| + C$

14. $a \ \frac{1}{\sqrt{15}}\arctan\frac{x}{\sqrt{15}} + \frac{1}{75}e^{75x} + C$

15. $a \ \frac{1}{21}(7x^2 + 5)^{\frac{3}{2}} + C$

16. $a \ 374$

17. $a \ 66.063$

18. $a \ 0$

19. $a \ 401$

20. *a* 24

21. *a* $\dfrac{\pi\sqrt{2}}{2}$

22. *a* 22

23. *a* $\dfrac{23}{2}$

24. *a* 20

25. *a* 9

26. *a* 30

27. *a* 14

28. *a* 219

29. *a* 766

30. *a* $\dfrac{79}{3}$

31. *a* 232.5

32. *a* 0

33. *a* $\dfrac{1}{3}e^{343} - \dfrac{1}{3}$

34. *a* $\dfrac{1}{2}(\ln(2))^2$

35. *a* $\sin(6) - \cos(6) - \sin(-3) + \cos(-3)$

36. *a* 0

37. *a* $7 + e^2$

38. *a* $\dfrac{364300}{3}$

39. *a* -2

40. *a* $\dfrac{\pi}{2}$

41. *a* $e^2 - e^{-5} + 35$

42. a $2e^2$

43. a -1

44. a $\dfrac{117}{3}e^2$

45. a $\dfrac{1}{7}e^{19} + \dfrac{1}{2}(\ln(2))^2 - \dfrac{1}{7}e^{12}$

46. a $\dfrac{575}{12}$

47. a $\dfrac{1}{6}e^6 + \dfrac{29}{6}$

48. a $\dfrac{1}{\pi}$

49. a $\dfrac{-3\ln\left(\frac{1}{2}\right)}{\pi}$

50. a $\pi^2 + \dfrac{2}{\pi}$

Chapter 6: Integrals Part II

Integration by Parts, Tabular Method, Special Trig Integrals,
Partial Fractions, Second Fundamental Theorem, Area
Between Curves, and Improper Integration

Integration by parts

Some complex integrals will require multiple steps to solve. This is most frequently seen when there is a product of two functions being integrated.

$$\int xe^x \, dx$$

The integral above cannot be solved using any of the basic integral formulas or a u-substitution.

The formula for integration by parts is given below.

$$\int u \, dv = uv - \int v \, du$$

The u expression for integration by parts should be chosen in the following order:

1. Logarithmic Function (ex. $\ln(x)$, $\log(x)$)
2. Inverse Trigonometric Functions (ex. $\arctan(x)$, $\arcsin(x)$)
3. Algebraic Expression (ex. x^2, x^7)
4. Trigonometric Expressions (ex. $\sin(x)$, $\cot(x)$)
5. Exponential Functions (ex. e^x, 2^x)

Once the u and dv expressions are chosen, take the derivative of the u function and the integral of the dv function. Plug in the calculated values into the formula for integration by parts.

6.1 $\int xe^x \, dx$

The correct u expression for this integral is x, and the corresponding dv expression is $e^x dx$.

$$u = x$$
$$dv = e^x dx$$

In order to obtain the pieces necessary for the integration by parts formula, we must take the derivative of the first equation, and the integral of the second equation. The constant of integration is not required when determining v, as it will be included in the final answer after integrating by parts.

$$\frac{du}{dx} = 1 \rightarrow du = dx$$

$$\int dv = \int e^x dx$$
$$v = e^x$$

Now that we have the necessary components for the integration by parts formula, substitution gives the form below.

$$x \cdot e^x - \int e^x \, dx$$

The integral of e^x is simply e^x.

$$\int xe^x \, dx = xe^x - e^x + C$$

6.2 $\int x \ln(x) \, dx$

The correct u expression is $\ln(x)$, and the correct dv expression is xdx.

$$u = \ln(x)$$
$$dv = x \cdot dx$$

Differentiating the first equation and integrating the second equation gives the equation below.

$$\frac{du}{dx} = \frac{1}{x} \rightarrow du = \frac{1}{x}dx$$

$$v = \frac{1}{2}x^2$$

Substituting into the integration by parts formula gives the answer below.

$$\ln(x) \cdot \frac{1}{2}x^2 - \int \frac{1}{2}x^2 \cdot \frac{1}{x}dx$$

$$\frac{x^2 \ln(x)}{2} - \frac{1}{2}\int x\, dx$$

$$\frac{x^2 \ln(x)}{2} - \frac{1}{4}x^2 + C$$

6.3 $\int e^x \sin(x)\, dx$

The correct u expression is $\sin(x)$ and the correct dv expression is $e^x dx$.

$$u = \sin(x)$$
$$dv = e^x dx$$

Differentiating the first equation, and integrating the second equation gives the equation below.

$$du = \cos(x)\, dx$$
$$v = e^x$$

Substituting into the integration by parts formula gives the form below.

$$\sin(x)\, e^x - \int e^x \cos(x)dx$$

At this point, the integral looks similar to the original problem. In order to fully solve the integral, it must be integrated by parts twice.

$$u = \cos(x)$$

$$dv = e^x dx$$

Differentiating the first equation and integrating the second equation gives the equation below.

$$du = -\sin(x)\,dx$$
$$v = e^x$$

$$\cos(x) \cdot e^x - \int e^x(-\sin(x))dx$$

Simplifying this expression gives the form below.

$$e^x \cos(x) + \int e^x \sin(x)dx$$

Inserting this expression for the integral expression in the first integration by parts gives the form below.

$$e^x \sin(x) - \left[e^x \cos(x) + \int e^x \sin(x)\,dx\right]$$

Simplifying this expression and setting it equal to the original problem gives the equation below.

$$\int e^x \sin(x)\,dx = e^x \sin(x) - e^x \cos(x) - \int e^x \sin(x)\,dx$$

Adding $\int e^x \sin(x)\,dx$ to both sides, we arrive at the form below.

$$2\int e^x \sin(x)\,dx = e^x \sin(x) - e^x \cos(x)$$

Finally, dividing both sides by 2 gives the final answer.

$$\int e^x \sin(x)\,dx = \frac{(e^x \sin(x) - e^x \cos(x))}{2} + C$$

Tabular Method of Integration

A special integration method when the u expression is algebraic is known as the tabular method of integration by parts. Begin by choosing the correct u and dv expressions. Next, set up a table with two columns. The left column will contain the derivatives of the u expression until the nth derivative equals 0. The right column will be of matching dimensions, containing the repeated integrations of the dv function with alternating signs.

6.4 $\displaystyle\int x^3 e^{2x}\, dx$

The appropriate u expression is x^3, and the appropriate dv expression is $e^x dx$. Since the u expression is algebraic, the tabular method can be used to solve this integral by parts more efficiently.

Differentiated u function	Integrated dv expression
x^3	e^{2x}
$3x^2$	$+\dfrac{1}{2}e^{2x}$
$6x$	$-\dfrac{1}{4}e^{2x}$
6	$+\dfrac{1}{8}e^{2x}$
0	$-\dfrac{1}{16}e^{2x}$

The arrows indicate that the functions are multiplied in the final answer of the integration by parts.

$$\int x^3 e^{2x}\, dx = \frac{1}{2}x^3 e^{2x} - \frac{3}{4}x^2 e^{2x} + \frac{3}{4}x e^{2x} - \frac{3}{8}e^{2x} + C$$

Special Trig Integrals

For integrals involving higher order trigonometric functions, it is often necessary to involve double angle identities and u-substitution. Some relevant trigonometric identities are listed in the table below.

Trigonometric Identities	
$\sin^2(x) + \cos^2(x)$	1
$\sin^2(x)$	$1 - \cos^2(x)$ or $\dfrac{1 - \cos(2x)}{2}$
$\cos^2(x)$	$1 - \sin^2(x)$ or $\dfrac{1 + \cos(2x)}{2}$
$\sin(2x)$	$2\sin(x)\cos(x)$
$\cos(2x)$	$2\cos^2(x) - 1$ or $1 - 2\sin^2(x)$ or $\cos^2(x) - \sin^2(x)$
$1 + \cot^2(x)$	$\csc^2(x)$
$\tan^2(x) + 1$	$\sec^2(x)$

6.5 $\displaystyle\int \sin^2(x)\,dx$

Rewrite the integrand in the form below.

$$\int \frac{1 - \cos(2x)}{2}\,dx$$

This integral can now be separated into two parts.

$$\int \frac{1}{2} dx - \frac{1}{2} \int \cos(2x) \, dx$$

Solving using the basic rules of integration and u-substitution, we arrive at the answer below.

$$\int \sin^2(x) \, dx = \frac{1}{2} x - \frac{1}{4} \sin(2x) + C$$

6.6 $\int \sin^3(x) \, dx$

Use the trigonometric identity $\sin^2(x) + \cos^2(x) = 1$ to simplify the integral.

$$\int (1 - \cos^2(x)) \, (\sin(x)) dx$$

Expand the integrand.

$$\int (\sin(x)) - \cos^2(x) \sin(x)) dx$$

Using the additive property of integrals, we arrive at the form below.

$$\int \sin(x) \, dx - \int \cos^2(x) \sin(x) \, dx$$

The first integral is equal to $-\cos(x)$, but the second integral will require a u-substitution.

$$u = \cos(x)$$

$$du = -\sin(x) \, dx$$

$$-\cos(x) - \left[- \int u^2\, du \right]$$

$$-\cos(x) + \frac{1}{3}\cos^3(x) + C$$

6.7 $\int \sin^2(x)\cos^2(x)\, dx$

Begin by using the power reduction identities for $\cos(x)$ to rewrite $\sin^2(x)$ and $\cos^2(x)$.

$$\int \left(\frac{1 - \cos(2x)}{2} \right) \left(\frac{(1 + \cos(2x))}{2} \right) dx$$

Simplifying the expression above gives the form below.

$$\frac{1}{4} \int 1 - \cos^2(2x)$$

Using the double angle identity again, the integral can be written in the form below.

$$\frac{1}{4} \int \left[1 - \left(\frac{1 + \cos(4x)}{2} \right) \right] dx$$

Using the properties of integrals, this expression can be simplified to the answer below.

$$\frac{1}{4} \int \left[\frac{1}{2} - \frac{1}{2}\cos(4x) \right] dx$$

$$\frac{1}{4} \left[\frac{1}{2}x - \frac{1}{8}\sin(4x) \right] + C$$

$$\frac{1}{8}x - \frac{1}{32}\sin(4x) + C$$

6.8 $\int \sec^4(x)\tan^4(x)\,dx$

Since the secant function is raised to an even power, the integrand can be rewritten in the form below.

$$\int \sec^2(x)\tan^4(x)\sec^2(x)\,dx$$

The appropriate u expression for this integral is $\tan(x)$.

$$u = \tan(x)$$

$$du = \sec^2(x)dx$$

Rewrite the integrand using a trigonometric identity.

$$\int (\tan^2(x)+1)(\tan^4(x))\sec^2(x)\,dx$$

Next, perform a u-substitution using $u = \tan(x)$.

$$\int (u^2+1)(u^4)du$$

Expand and solve the integral.

$$\int (u^6+u^4)\,du$$

$$\frac{1}{7}u^7 + \frac{1}{5}u^5 + C$$

Replace u with $\tan(x)$.

$$\frac{1}{7}\tan^7(x) + \frac{1}{5}\tan^5(x) + C$$

6.9 $\displaystyle\int \sec^3(x)\tan^3(x)\,dx$

Since the secant function is raised to the odd power, the integrand can be written in the form below.

$$\int \sec^2(x)\tan^2(x)\sec(x)\tan(x)\,dx$$

This can be rewritten using a u-substitution using $u = \sec(x)$.

$$u = \sec(x)$$

$$du = \sec(x)\tan(x)\,dx$$

Rewrite the integral in terms of $\sec(x)$ using the trigonometric identity.

$$\int [(\sec^2(x) - 1)(\sec^2(x))\sec(x)\tan(x)]\,dx$$

$$\int [(\sec^4(x) - \sec^2(x))\sec(x)\tan(x)]\,dx$$

Perform the u-substitution.

$$\int (u^4 - u^2)\,du$$

Use the power rule of integrals to solve.

$$\frac{1}{5}u^5 - \frac{1}{3}u^3 + C$$

Replace u with $\sec(x)$.

$$\frac{1}{5}\sec^5(x) - \frac{1}{3}\sec^3(x) + C$$

6.10 $\int \tan^3(x)\, dx$

Rewrite the expression in the form below.

$$\int (\sec^2(x) - 1)(\tan(x))\, dx$$

By simplifying, we arrive at the form below.

$$\int (\sec^2(x)\tan(x) - \tan(x))\, dx$$

Then using the u-substitution below, the first portion of the integral can be solved.

$$u = \sec(x)$$

$$du = \sec(x)\tan(x)$$

$$\int u\, du - \int \tan(x)\, dx$$

Using the basic integral rules and the special integral for $\tan(x)$, we arrive at the form below.

$$\frac{1}{2}u^2 - (-\ln|\cos(x)|) + C$$

Replace u with $\sec(x)$.

$$\frac{1}{2}\sec^2(x) + \ln|\cos(x)| + C$$

Partial Fractions

A handy trick to solve more complex integrals is to decompose rational integrands as the sum of two or more fractions. In order to accomplish this, follow the guidelines outlined below:

Partial Fraction Assumptions	
Linear Factors $$\frac{f(x)}{(x+a)(x+b)}$$	$$\frac{A}{x+a} + \frac{B}{x+b}$$
Repeated Linear Factors $$\frac{f(x)}{(x+a)^3}$$	$$\frac{A}{x+a} + \frac{B}{(x+a)^2} + \frac{C}{(x+a)^3}$$
Quadratic /Polynomial Term $$\frac{f(x)}{(ax^2+bx+c)(dx+e)}$$	$$\frac{Ax+B}{ax^2+bx+c} + \frac{C}{dx+e}$$

The partial fraction assumptions are not limited to the ones shown in the table above. After choosing the appropriate partial fraction assumption, set the integrand expression equal to the assumption. Solve for the constants A, B, C, etc., by using a system of equations or pairing coefficient values.

6.11 $\int \dfrac{1}{(x^2 + 3x + 2)}\, dx$

Choose the correct assumption for the partial fraction, and set it equal to the integrand expression.

$$\frac{1}{x^2 + 3x + 2} = \frac{A}{(x+1)} + \frac{B}{(x+2)}$$

Begin solving for A and B by using a common denominator.

$$\frac{1}{x^2 + 3x + 2} = \frac{A(x+2)}{(x+1)(x+2)} + \frac{B(x+1)}{(x+2)(x+1)}$$

Since the denominators are all equivalent, the numerators can be equated as follows.

$$1 = A(x+2) + B(x+1)$$

To solve for B, x can be set as -2.

$$1 = A(-2+2) + B(-2+1)$$

$$1 = 0 + (-B)$$

$$B = -1$$

To solve for A, x can be set as -1.

$$1 = A(-1+2) + B(-1+1)$$

$$1 = A + 0$$

$$A = 1$$

The values of A and B can now be replaced in the original partial fraction assumption.

$$\frac{1}{(x+1)} + \frac{-1}{(x+2)}$$

To ensure that this is the correct partial fraction decomposition, we can add the two fractions above by cross-multiplying.

$$\frac{x+2}{x^2 + 3x + 2} + \frac{-x-1}{x^2 + 3x + 2} = \frac{1}{x^2 + 3x + 2}$$

Since the partial fraction decomposition is valid, the original integral can be rewritten in the form below.

$$\int \left(\frac{1}{x+1} - \frac{1}{x+2} \right) dx$$

This integral can now be solved using the natural logarithm.

$$\ln|x+1| - \ln|x+2| + C$$

6.12 $\int \dfrac{2x}{(x+2)^2} dx$

Choose the correct assumption for the partial fraction decomposition as shown below.

$$\frac{2x}{(x+2)^2} = \frac{A}{x+2} + \frac{B}{(x+2)^2}$$

Find a common denominator for all the fractions.

$$\frac{2x}{(x+2)^2} = \frac{A(x+2)}{(x+2)^2} + \frac{B}{(x+2)^2}$$

Set the numerators equal to each other.

$$2x = A(x+2) + B$$

Set $x = -2$ to solve for B.

$$-4 = A(0) + B$$

$$B = -4$$

Replace the value of B in the step above in order to solve for A.

$$2x = A(x+2) - 4$$

Set $x = 1$ and solve for A.

$$2 = 3A - 4$$

$$A = 2$$

Substitute the values of A and B into the partial fraction decomposition.

$$\int \left(\frac{2}{x+2} + \frac{-4}{(x+2)^2} \right) dx$$

This function can now be integrated easily using the basic integral formulas.

$$2 \ln|x+2| + 4(x+2)^{-1} + C$$

6.13 $\int \dfrac{4}{x^3 + x^2 + x + 1} dx$

Choose the correct assumption for the partial fraction decomposition after factoring the denominator.

$$\frac{4}{(x^2+1)(x+1)} = \frac{Ax+B}{x^2+1} + \frac{C}{x+1}$$

Find the common denominator for the three fractions as follows.

$$\frac{4}{(x^2+1)(x+1)} = \frac{(Ax+B)(x+1)}{(x^2+1)(x+1)} + \frac{C(x^2+1)}{(x+1)(x^2+1)}$$

This can be simplified by removing the denominators and expanding.

$$4 = Ax^2 + Ax + Bx + B + Cx^2 + C$$

Rather than choosing arbitrary values for x in order to solve for the coefficients, we can rewrite the equation and solve by pairing coefficient values.

$$0x^2 + 0x + 4 = (A + C)x^2 + (B + A)x + (B + C)$$

Now, a simultaneous equation can easily be solved (using any method) to determine the value of each coefficient.

$$A + C = 0$$
$$B + A = 0$$
$$B + C = 4$$

$$A = -2, B = 2, C = 2$$

Replacing the values found from the system above into the original partial fraction decomposition results in the form below.

$$\frac{4}{(x^2 + 1)(x + 1)} = \frac{-2x + 2}{x^2 + 1} + \frac{2}{x + 1}$$

This makes the integrand much easier to evaluate.

$$\int \left(-\frac{2x}{x^2 + 1} + \frac{2}{x^2 + 1} + \frac{2}{x + 1} \right) dx$$

$$-\ln|x^2 + 1| + 2\arctan(x) + 2\ln|x + 1| + C$$

Second Fundamental Theorem

The second fundamental theorem of calculus helps connect the concepts of integrals and derivatives. For a function $f(x)$ continuous on the interval $[a, b]$, the second fundamental theorem is stated below.

$$\frac{d}{dx}\left(\int_a^x f(t)dt \right) = f(x)$$

where x is between a and b.

A more general statement of the second fundamental theorem, for upper bounds not having a derivative of 1 is given as follows.

$$\frac{d}{dx}\left(\int_a^{g(x)} f(t)dt \right) = f(g(x)) \cdot g'(x)$$

This means that after substituting the upper bound function into the integrand, it must be multiplied by its derivative. An example of this is shown below (6.15).

6.14 $\frac{d}{dx}\left(\int_0^x (t^2 + t + 1)dt \right)$

Substitute the value of x into the function $f(t)$ as follows.

$$x^2 + x + 1$$

6.15 $\frac{d}{dx}\left(\int_0^{x^2} \sin(t)\, dt \right)$

Substitute the value of x^2 into the integrand expression, then multiply by the derivative.

6.16 $\dfrac{d}{dx}\left(\displaystyle\int\limits_{0}^{\cos(x)} \sin^2(x)\right)$ $\qquad \sin(x^2)\cdot 2x$

Substitute the value of $\cos(x)$ into the integrand expression and multiply by the derivative.

$$\sin^2(\cos(x))\cdot(-\sin(x))$$

By simplifying, we arrive at the answer below.

$$-\sin^2(\cos(x))\cdot\sin(x)$$

Area Between Curves

A useful application of integration is to determine the bounded region between two functions on a given interval. The area between the curves $y = f(x)$ and $y = g(x)$ on the interval $[a, b]$, assuming that $f(x) \geq g(x)$, is written in the form below.

$$A = \int_a^b [f(x) - g(x)]dx$$

6. 17 Determine the area between the functions $f(x) = x^2$ and $g(x) = x^3$ on the interval $[1,3]$.

The area between the curves x^2 and x^3 on the interval $[1,3]$ is shown in the graph below.

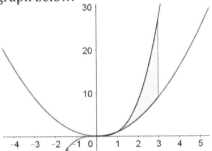

On this interval, x^3 is greater than x^2. Therefore, the area between the two curves can be calculated using the first fundamental theorem of calculus.

$$A = \int_1^3 (x^3 - x^2)dx$$

$$\left[\frac{1}{4}x^4 - \frac{1}{3}x^3 \right]_1^3$$

$$A = \left[\frac{1}{4}(81) - \frac{1}{3}(27) \right] - \left[\frac{1}{4} - \frac{1}{3} \right] = \frac{34}{3}$$

6.18 Determine the area enclosed by the functions $x = y^2 - 3$ and $y = x + 1$.

A graph of the two functions is shown below.

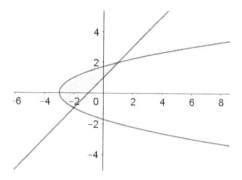

In order to find the intersection points, the two functions can be equated as follows.

$$y = y^2 - 3 + 1$$

$$y = y^2 - 2$$

$$y^2 - y - 2 = 0$$

$$(y + 1)(y - 2) = 0$$

$$y = -1, y = 2$$

The values found above indicate the bounds for the area enclosed on the y-axis. Thus the integral for the enclosed region can be written in the form below.

$$A = \int_{-1}^{2} [(y - 1) - (y^2 - 3)] \, dy$$

Notice that this integral is written in terms of y, and therefore includes the expression dy in the integrand. When solving for bounded areas using functions of y, remember that the integrand is equal to the function on the right minus the function on the left.

Solving the integral for the area between the functions, we arrive at the answer below.

$$\int_{-1}^{2}(-y^2 + y + 2)dy$$

$$\left[-\frac{1}{3}y^3 + \frac{1}{2}y^2 + 2y\right]_{-1}^{2}$$

$$\left(-\frac{8}{3} + 2 + 4\right) - \left(\frac{1}{3} + \frac{1}{2} - 2\right)$$

$$A = 4.5$$

6.19 Determine the area enclosed by $f(x) = \cos(x)$ and $g(x) = \sin(x)$ on the interval $\left[0, \frac{\pi}{2}\right]$.

The graph below shows the area between the two functions that we are trying to find.

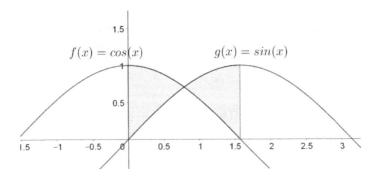

Notice that there is an intersection point at $x = \frac{\pi}{4}$ in the interval that we are working with. This means the integral expression for the area between the curves will need to be written as two separate integrals.

$$A = \int_{0}^{\frac{\pi}{4}} (\cos(x) - \sin(x))\, dx + \int_{\frac{\pi}{4}}^{\frac{\pi}{2}} (\sin(x) - \cos(x))\, dx$$

Solving the integral and then applying the first fundamental theorem, we arrive at the answer below.

$$[\sin(x) + \cos(x)]_{0}^{\frac{\pi}{4}} + [-\cos(x) - \sin(x)]_{\frac{\pi}{4}}^{\frac{\pi}{2}}$$

$$(\sqrt{2} - 1) + (-1 + \sqrt{2})$$

$$A = 2\sqrt{2} - 2$$

Improper Integrals

An integral with one or more interval bounds equal to infinity or infinite at a point along the interval of integration, is known as an improper integral.

In order to solve an improper integral and determine the area under the curve, replace the infinite bound with another variable, and determine the value of the integral as this new variable approaches infinity. This is done using a limit as the variable approaches an infinite value. The table below shows some of the properties of indefinite integrals that can be used when solving problems.

Basic Indefinite Integral Properties
$$\int_{a}^{\infty} f(x)\,dx = \lim_{b \to \infty} \int_{a}^{b} f(x)\,dx$$
$$\int_{-\infty}^{b} f(x)\,dx = \lim_{a \to -\infty} \int_{a}^{b} f(x)\,dx$$
$$\int_{-\infty}^{\infty} f(x)\,dx = \int_{-\infty}^{c} f(x)\,dx + \int_{c}^{\infty} f(x)\,dx$$ Where c is any number, and both of the integrals are convergent.

6.20 $\displaystyle\int_{1}^{\infty} \frac{1}{x^3}\,dx$

Begin by solving the integral using the power rule of integration.

$$\left[-\frac{1}{2}x^{-2}\right]_{1}^{\infty}$$

Since the value of ∞ cannot be substituted into the first fundamental theorem, rewrite the upper bound as b, and calculate the $\lim_{b\to\infty} F(x)$ as follows.

$$\lim_{b\to\infty}\left[-\frac{1}{2}x^{-2}\right]_{1}^{b}$$

Using the first fundamental theorem, we arrive at the form below.

$$\lim_{b\to\infty}\left[-\frac{1}{2}b^{-2} - \left(-\frac{1}{2}\cdot 1^{-2}\right)\right]$$

$$\lim_{b\to\infty}\left[-\frac{1}{2}b^{-2} + \frac{1}{2}\right] = 0 + \frac{1}{2} = \frac{1}{2}$$

6.21 $\displaystyle\int_{-\infty}^{0} \frac{1}{1+x^2}\,dx$

This indefinite integral can be rewritten in the form below.

$$\lim_{a\to -\infty}\int_{a}^{0} \frac{1}{1+x^2}\,dx$$

Performing the integration results in the form below.

$$\lim_{a\to -\infty}\left[\arctan(x)\right]_{a}^{0}$$

Using the first fundamental theorem, we arrive at the form below.

$$\lim_{a \to -\infty} [\arctan(0) - \arctan(a)]$$

Since $\arctan(0) = 0$, and the $\lim_{a \to -\infty} \arctan(x) = -\frac{\pi}{2}$, the area under the curve is equal to the following.

$$\left[0 - \left(-\frac{\pi}{2}\right)\right] = \frac{\pi}{2}$$

6.22 $\displaystyle\int_{-\infty}^{\infty} (-4x^3 e^{-x^4})dx$

This improper integral can be rewritten in the form below.

$$\int_{-\infty}^{0} (-4x^3 e^{-x^4})dx + \int_{0}^{\infty} (-4x^3 e^{-x^4})dx$$

Changing the bounds of the integrals to a limit, we arrive at the form below.

$$\lim_{a \to -\infty} \int_{a}^{0} (-4x^3 e^{-x^4})dx + \lim_{b \to \infty} \int_{0}^{b} (-4x^3 e^{-x^4})dx$$

Using a u-substitution, the indefinite integral of the function is of the form below.

$$\int (-4x^3 e^{-x^4})dx = e^{-x^4} + C$$

Therefore, the indefinite integral can be written in the form below.

$$\lim_{a \to -\infty} \left[e^{-x^4} \right]_a^0 + \lim_{b \to \infty} \left[e^{-x^4} \right]_0^b$$

The first fundamental theorem results in the form below.

$$\lim_{a \to -\infty} \left[1 - e^{-a^4} \right] + \lim_{b \to \infty} \left[e^{-b^4} - 1 \right]$$

The limit as $-e^{-a^4}$ approaches negative infinity is 0, and the limit as e^{-b^4} is also zero. Therefore the area under the curve on the interval $(-\infty, \infty)$ is 0.

6. 23 $\displaystyle\int_1^\infty \frac{1}{x} dx$

The improper integral can be rewritten in the form below.

$$\lim_{b \to \infty} \int_1^b \frac{1}{x} dx$$

Solving the integral using the natural logarithm, we arrive at the form below.

$$\lim_{b \to \infty} \left[\ln(x) \right]_1^b$$

Using the first fundamental theorem, we arrive at the form below.

$$\lim_{b \to \infty} \left[\ln(b) - \ln(1) \right]$$

The limit as b approaches infinity for the function $\ln(b)$ is equal to infinity. Therefore the expression above can be written as $\infty - 0$. This means that the area under the curve diverges and cannot be determined.

6.24 $\displaystyle\int_{0}^{1} \frac{1}{\sqrt{1-x}}\,dx$

At the point $x = 1$, the function is not defined. The improper integral can be rewritten in the form below.

$$\lim_{b \to 1^-} \int_{0}^{b} \frac{1}{\sqrt{1-x}}\,dx$$

Using a u-substition to take the integral of the function results in the form below.

$$\lim_{b \to 1^-} \left[-2\sqrt{1-x}\right]_{0}^{b}$$

Applying the first fundamental theorem, we arrive at the form below.

$$\lim_{b \to 1^-} \left[2\sqrt{1-b} - (-2)\right]$$

The limit of $\sqrt{1-b}$ as b approaches 1 from the negative x-axis is equal to zero. Therefore the area under the curve is shown below.

$$0 - (-2) = 2$$

You can find practice problems for this chapter beginning on the next page.

Chapter 6 Practice Problems

Evaluate the following

1. $\int \arctan(x)\, dx$

2. $\int x^3 e^{3x}\, dx$

3. $\int \sin^2(x) \cos(x)\, dx$

4. $\int \ln(x)\, dx$

5. $\int e^x \cos(x)\, dx$

6. $\int x^4 e^x\, dx$

7. $\int x\sqrt{x-4}\, dx$

8. $\int 2x \cdot \sin(x)\, dx$

9. $\int \arcsin(x)\, dx$

10. $\int x \cdot \ln(x)\, dx$

11. $\int \cos^5(x)\, dx$

12. $\int \sin^3(x)\, dx$

13. $\displaystyle\int \sec^2(x) \tan^3(x)\, dx$

14. $\displaystyle\int \sec^7(x) \tan(x)\, dx$

15. $\displaystyle\int \sec^4(x) \tan^2(x)\, dx$

16. $\displaystyle\int \csc^2(x) \cot^2(x)\, dx$

17. $\displaystyle\int \cos^2(x)\, dx$

18. $\displaystyle\int \sin^2(2x) \cos(x)\, dx$

19. $\displaystyle\int \cos^4(x)\, dx$

20. $\displaystyle\int \frac{\cos^2(x)}{\sin^2(x)\cos(x)}\, dx$

21. $\displaystyle\int \frac{1}{x^2 + 4x + 3}\, dx$

22. $\displaystyle\int \frac{2}{x(x+2)^2}\, dx$

23. $\displaystyle\int \frac{1}{(x^2 - 4)}\, dx$

24. $\displaystyle\int \frac{60}{x(x+3)(x+4)(x+5)}\, dx$

25. $\displaystyle\int \frac{2}{(x^2 + 6x + 8)(x+1)}\, dx$

26. $\int \dfrac{3}{(x+3)^3} \, dx$

27. $\int \dfrac{1}{(x^3 + 3x^2 + 3x + 9)} \, dx$

28. $\int \dfrac{5x}{(x+1)(x+3)} \, dx$

29. $\int \dfrac{x^2 + 3x}{x^2 - 1} \, dx$

30. $\int \dfrac{4x + 7}{(x+3)^3} \, dx$

31. $\dfrac{d}{dx} \left(\displaystyle\int_0^x \tan^2(2t) \, dt \right)$

32. $\dfrac{d}{dx} \left(\displaystyle\int_0^{\cos(x) \cdot \sin(x)} (3t) \, dt \right)$

33. $\dfrac{d}{dx} \left(\displaystyle\int_0^{(x+7)(x+3)^2} (t^2) \, dt \right)$

34. $\dfrac{d}{dx} \left(\displaystyle\int_0^{\frac{(x+2)^2}{(x-7)^3}} \cos(t) \, dt \right)$

35. $\dfrac{d}{dx} \left(\displaystyle\int_0^{x \ln(x)} (\tan(t) + \sin(t)) \, dt \right)$

36. Find the area bounded by the functions $f(x) = x^2 + 3x + 2$ and $g(x) = x + 5$.

37. Find the area bounded by the functions $f(x) = \cos(x)$ and $g(x) = x^2 + 3x$ on the interval $[\pi, 2\pi]$.

38. Find the area bounded by the functions $f(x) = \sqrt{x}$ and $g(x) = e^x$ on the interval $[1,5]$.

39. Find the area bounded by the functions $f(x) = \sec^2(x)$ and $g(x) = \tan(x)$ on the interval $\left[0, \frac{\pi}{4}\right]$.

40. Find the area bounded by $x = y^2$ and $-y^2 + 8 = x$.

41. $\displaystyle\int_{1}^{\infty} \frac{1}{x^5} dx$

42. $\displaystyle\int_{-\infty}^{1} \frac{1}{1+x^2} dx$

43. $\displaystyle\int_{0}^{8} \frac{1}{\sqrt{8-x}} dx$

44. $\displaystyle\int_{0}^{\infty} x^3 e^{-x^4} dx$

45. $\displaystyle\int_{-\infty}^{\infty} \arctan(x)\, dx$

46. $\displaystyle\int_{-\infty}^{-1} \frac{1}{x^2} dx$

47. $\displaystyle\int_{1}^{\infty} \frac{1}{x}\,dx$

48. $\displaystyle\int_{-\infty}^{\infty} xe^{x}\,dx$

49. $\displaystyle\int_{-5}^{2} \frac{(x+1)^2}{(x+1)}\,dx$

50. $\displaystyle\int_{1}^{\infty} \frac{1}{x\ln(x)}\,dx$

Chapter 6 Practice Problem Answers

1. $a \; x \cdot \arctan(x) - \frac{1}{2}\ln|x^2 + 1| + C$

2. $a \; \frac{1}{3}x^3 e^{3x} - \frac{1}{3}x^2 e^{3x} + \frac{2}{9}xe^{3x} - \frac{2}{27}e^{3x} + C$

3. $a \; \frac{1}{3}\sin^3(x) + C$

4. $a \; x \cdot \ln(x) - x + C$

5. $a \; \frac{1}{2}e^x \cdot \sin(x) + \frac{1}{2}e^x \cdot \cos(x) + C$

6. $a \; x^4 e^x - 4x^3 e^x + 12x^2 e^x - 24xe^x + 24e^x + C$

7. $a \; \frac{2x}{3}(x-4)^{\frac{3}{2}} - \frac{4}{15}(x-4)^{\frac{5}{2}} + C$

8. $a \; 2\sin(x) - 2x \cdot \cos(x) + C$

9. $a \; x \cdot \arcsin(x) + \sqrt{1-x^2} + C$

10. $a \; \frac{1}{2}x^2 \ln(x) - \frac{1}{4}x^2 + C$

11. $a \; \frac{1}{5}\sin^5(x) - \frac{2}{3}\sin^3(x) + \sin(x) + C$

12. $a \; \frac{1}{3}\cos^3(x) - \cos(x) + C$

13. $a \; \frac{1}{4}\tan^4(x) + C$

14. $a \; \frac{1}{7}\sec^7(x) + C$

15. $a \; \frac{1}{5}\tan^5(x) + \frac{1}{3}\tan^3(x) + C$

16. $a \; -\frac{1}{3}\cot^3(x) + C$

17. $a \; \frac{1}{4}\sin(2x) + \frac{1}{2}x + C$

18. $a \; \frac{4}{3}\sin^3(x) - \frac{4}{5}\sin^5(x) + C$

19. $a \; \frac{1}{32}\sin(4x) + \frac{1}{4}\sin(2x) + \frac{3}{8}x + C$

20. $a \; -\csc(x) + C$

21. a $\frac{1}{2}\ln|x+1| - \frac{1}{2}\ln|x+3| + C$

22. a $\frac{1}{2}\ln|x| - \frac{1}{2}\ln|x+2| + \frac{1}{x+2} + C$

23. a $\frac{1}{4}\ln|x-2| - \frac{1}{4}\ln|x+2| + C$

24. a $-6\ln|x+5| + 15\ln|x+4| - 10\ln|x+3| + \ln|x| + C$

25. a $\frac{1}{3}\ln|x+4| + \frac{2}{3}\ln|x+1| - \ln|x+2| + C$

26. a $-\frac{3}{2(x+3)^2} + C$

27. a $\frac{1}{12}\ln|x+3| - \frac{1}{24}\ln|x^2+3| + \frac{\sqrt{3}}{12}\arctan\left(\frac{x}{\sqrt{3}}\right) + C$

28. a $\frac{15}{2}\ln|x+3| - \frac{5}{2}\ln|x+1| + C$

29. a $\ln|x+1| + x + 2\ln|x-1| + C$

30. a $\frac{5}{2(x+3)^2} - \frac{4}{x+3} + C$

31. a $\tan^2(2x)$

32. a $3\cos(x)\sin(x)\cdot\cos(2x)$

33. u $\left((x+7)(x+3)^2\right)^2 \cdot (3x^2 + 26x + 51)$

34. a $\cos\left(\frac{(x+2)^2}{(x-7)^3}\right)\cdot\frac{-(x+20)(x+2)}{(x-7)^4}$

35. a $(\tan(x\ln(x)) + \sin(x\ln(x)))\cdot(\ln(x) + 1)$

36. a $\frac{32}{3}$

37. a $\frac{7}{3}\pi^3 + \frac{9}{2}\pi^2$

38. a $e^5 - \frac{2}{3}\cdot 5^{\frac{3}{2}} - e + \frac{2}{3}$

39. a $1 + \ln\left(\frac{\sqrt{2}}{2}\right)$

40. a $\frac{64}{3}$

41. $a \frac{1}{4}$

42. $a \frac{3\pi}{4}$

43. $a \ 2^{\frac{5}{2}}$

44. $a \frac{1}{4}$

45. $a \ 0$

46. $a \ 1$

47. a Diverges/Infinite

48. a Diverges/Infinite

49. $a \ -\frac{7}{2}$

50. a Diverges/Infinite

Chapter 7: Applications of Calculus Principles

Parametric Equations, Motion, Related Rates, and Volumes of Solids

Parametric Equations

Parametric equations are the typical xy equations defined by another, 3rd, variable. This variable is usually defined by t, which is often used to represent time, as can be seen later in this chapter.

One thing you may be asked to do with parametric equations is identify the graph in the xy plane. This is done by a simple arithmetic method called eliminating the parameter. Look at the example below.

7.1 What do the parametric equations below represent?

$x = \sin(t), y = \cos(t)$

Recall how $\sin^2(t) + \cos^2(t) = 1$. The equations then represent a circle of radius 1, defined by the equation below.

$$x^2 + y^2 = 1$$

7.2 What do the parametric equations below represent?

$x = 2t, y = t^2$

For this problem, we must isolate for the parameter, t.

$$t = \frac{x}{2} = \pm\sqrt{y}$$

This then can be simplified, by ignoring the parameter.

$$y = \left(\frac{x}{2}\right)^2$$

This means that the parametric equations represent a parabola.

Derivatives of parametric functions are somewhat different from explicit functions in x and y. The derivatives for a parametric function are of the form on the following page.

$$\frac{dy}{dx} = \frac{\frac{dy}{dt}}{\frac{dx}{dt}}$$

The derivative of the parametric of y divided by the derivative of the parametric of x results in the derivative of y with respect to x. This gets a little trickier when the second derivative is needed.

$$\frac{dy^2}{d^2x} = \frac{\frac{d\left(\frac{dy}{dx}\right)}{dt}}{\frac{dx}{dt}}$$

Notice how the first derivative must be derived with respect to t and then must be divided by derivative of the parametric equation of x.

7.3 Identify the first and second derivatives for the parametric equations below.

$x = \sin(3t), y = 4\cos(3t)$

$$\frac{dy}{dx} = \frac{\frac{dy}{dt}}{\frac{dx}{dt}} = \frac{-12\sin(3t)}{3\cos(3t)} = -\frac{16x}{y}$$

You may be asked to simplify the parametric into terms of only x and y, as done above.

$$\frac{dy^2}{d^2x} = \frac{(3\cos(3t))(-36\cos(3t)) - (-12\sin(3t))(-9\sin(3t))}{(3\cos(3t))^2 \cdot (3\cos(3t))}$$

This can be simplified to the form below.

$$\frac{dy^2}{d^2x} = -\frac{108}{27\cos^3(3t)} = -\frac{108}{27\left(\frac{y}{4}\right)^3} = -256y^{-3}$$

This can also be determined by eliminating the parameter and taking the derivative implicitly.

$$x^2 + \left(\frac{y}{4}\right)^2 = x^2 + \frac{y^2}{16} = 1$$

$$2x + \frac{y}{8} \cdot \frac{dy}{dx} = 0$$

$$\frac{dy}{dx} = -\frac{16x}{y}$$

$$\frac{dy^2}{d^2x} = -\frac{y(16) - (16x)\left(\frac{dy}{dx}\right)}{y^2} = \frac{-16y^2 - 256x^2}{y^3} = -256y^{-3}$$

Although some algebraic work was necessary to determine that the two were equivalent, it is clear that either method will result in the proper derivatives of the parametric equations.

Another thing you may be asked to do with parametric functions and derivation is to find the points of horizontal and vertical tangency.

A horizontal tangent exists when $\frac{dy}{dt} = 0$ and $\frac{dx}{dt} \neq 0$.

A vertical tangent exists when $\frac{dx}{dt} = 0$ and $\frac{dy}{dt} \neq 0$.

Using the example 7.3, vertical and horizontal tangents exist at the values below.

$$\frac{dy}{dt} = -12\sin(3t) = 0$$

$$t = \frac{\pi k}{3}$$

Where k is any integer.

$$\frac{dx}{dt} = 3\cos(3t) = 0$$

$$t = \frac{\pi}{6} \pm \frac{\pi k}{3}$$

Where k is any integer.

This means that horizontal tangents exist where $t = \frac{\pi k}{3}$, and vertical tangents exist where $t = \frac{\pi}{6} + \frac{\pi k}{3}$, as these two values of t can never be equivalent. For the domain below, the values would be of the form below.

Vertical tangents: $t = \frac{\pi}{6}, \frac{\pi}{2}, \frac{5\pi}{6}, \frac{7\pi}{6}, \frac{3\pi}{2}, \frac{11\pi}{6}, 0 < -t \leq 2\pi$

Horizontal tangents: $t = \frac{\pi}{3}, \frac{2\pi}{3}, \pi, \frac{4\pi}{3}, \frac{5\pi}{3}, 2\pi, \; 0 < -t \leq 2\pi$

Parametric equations can also be written in vector form.

$$r(t) = \langle f(t), g(t) \rangle$$

Where $f(t) = x$ and $g(t) = y$. This is the same principle as a parametric equation, just written in a different form.

The derivative of a vector is merely the derivative of each of its components, so the derivative is of the form below.

$$r'(t) = \langle f'(t), g'(t) \rangle$$

Where $r'(t) = \langle x'(t), y'(t) \rangle = \langle \frac{dx}{dt}, \frac{dy}{dt} \rangle$.

All of the uses of parametric functions apply to vector-value functions as well. The same processes would be used to solve problems using either form.

Motion

The derivative tool of mathematics is very useful in physics application.

If we have a function, $s(x)$, which describes the position of an object in space, we can determine the acceleration and velocity functions of the object's movement.

If we take the derivative of the position function, we get the velocity function, $v(x)$.

$$s'(x) = v(x)$$

If we then derive the position function a second time, or derive the velocity function, then the acceleration function, $a(x)$, for the object is the result.

$$s''(x) = v'(x) = a(x)$$

This pattern between an object's position, velocity, and acceleration is very important and should be put to memory. This pattern is true regardless of the form of the position, whether it be given in vector, parametric, or any other form.

7. 5 Identify the velocity and acceleration functions of the particle moving according to the position function below.

$$s(t) = 4t^3 + 3\ln(t)$$

The velocity and acceleration functions would be of the form below.

$$s'(t) = v(t) = 12t^2 + \frac{3}{t}$$

$$v'(t) = a(t) = 24t - \frac{3}{t^2}$$

It is important to remember that these functions can be defined by vectors, parameters, or any other form. The same principles apply, regardless of the functions' form.

Another important topic for parametric and vector equations is arc length. This is often important for finding the total distance a particle traveled using the derivative of its motion.

The formula for arc length in parametric or vector form can be seen below.

$$L = \int_a^b \sqrt{\left(\frac{dx}{dt}\right)^2 + \left(\frac{dy}{dt}\right)^2}\, dt$$

Where a and b are values of t.

You may be asked to find the distance a particle has traveled for a given position function. While this can be done using arc length, the formula below is much simpler.

$$\text{Distance} = \int_a^b |v(t)|\, dt$$

However, you may also be asked to find the displacement, which is the change of an object's position from an initial position. Displacement is not always equivalent to the distance traveled by a particle. For example, a particle can take a long path with lots of distance only to return to its original position.

The displacement can be found using the formula below.

$$\text{Displacement} = \int_a^b v(t)\, dt$$

You may also be asked to determine the speed of the particle at any moment in time. The speed of a particle is equal to the magnitude of its velocity vector at a given time. This means, that the length of the velocity vector at a given time is equal to the speed of the particle at that time.

$$s = |v(t)|$$

Where s is speed and $v(t)$ is the velocity vector.

It is important to remember that velocity has a speed and a direction, meaning that it shows more than just the rate of travel of a particle.

It is also important to be able to recognize when the speed of a particle is increasing or decreasing.

The speed of a particle does not simply increase with an increase or decrease in the velocity function, but also depends on the acceleration function.

When the acceleration and the velocity are both positive or both negative, then the speed of the particle is increasing.

When the acceleration and the velocity have opposite signs, meaning that the acceleration is positive while the velocity is negative or vice versa, then the speed of the particle is decreasing.

Related Rates

Related Rate problems occur when two objects are in motion that are related to one another. There is no set formula or pattern for solving related rate problems. However, the setup below may help in solving problems of this nature.

Related Rates Setup
Necessary tools:
A Relation Between the Two Differentials
A Rate of Change
A Picture or Graphic (Sometimes)
A Specific Input Value
Solving Steps:
1. Determine a Relationship Between the Given Values
2. Take the Derivative of the Relationship Implicitly
3. Plug in Known Values
4. Identify Solution

7.6 Sand is pouring out of a bag at a constant rate of 4 $cm^3 s^{-1}$, which forms a conical pile on the ground beneath the bag. The cone has a radius that is equal to its height. Identify the rate of change of the radius of the cone when its radius is 2 cm.

First, we need a relation, or some relationship between the different pieces of given information.

The volume of a cone is of the form below.

$$V = \frac{1}{3}\pi r^2 h$$

This will be our relation for this problem. It is also important to recognize that the rate of the sand exiting the bag is equivalent to the rate of change of the volume of the cone. Each grain of sand that adds to the pile adds volume to the cone.

$$\frac{dv}{dt} = 4$$

Now that we have all the different necessary pieces, we can begin the problem.

First, we take the derivative of the relation, which can be seen below.

$$\frac{dv}{dt} = \frac{2}{3}\pi rh \cdot \frac{dr}{dt} + \frac{1}{3}\pi r^2 \cdot \frac{dh}{dt}$$

As $h = r, \frac{dr}{dt} = \frac{dh}{dt}$, which means the volume differential can be simplified to the form below.

$$\frac{dv}{dt} = \frac{dr}{dt}\left(\frac{2}{3}r^2\pi + \frac{1}{3}\pi r^2\right)$$

Now we must plug in all the known values. This can be seen below.

$$\frac{dv}{dt} = 4 = \frac{dr}{dt}\left(\frac{2}{3}(2)^2\pi + \frac{1}{3}\pi(2)^2\right) = \frac{dr}{dt}(4\pi)$$

The rate of change of the radius and height of the cone is then of the form below.

$$\frac{dr}{dt} = \frac{1}{\pi} \text{ cm s}^{-1}$$

Don't forget to put units. While this problem may seem easy as it is worked through, related rate problems can often present difficult challenges for calculus students. However, using the steps and pattern given in this book, any related rates problems can be solved.

Although it was not necessary for the example problem, often a drawing or sketch of the given scenario can help in identifying the relationship between the different parts of the problem.

Volumes of Revolution

In the integrals chapter, we identified how to find the area underneath a curve and between curves. What if we used the integral to calculate the volume of a 3-dimensional object?

7.7 Observe the function $y = x$ on the domain $0 \leq x \leq 4$

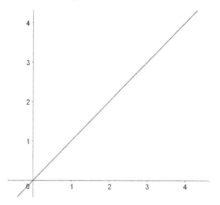

If the function were revolved around the x-axis, a cone of radius y would result. This can be seen below.

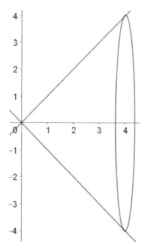

We can calculate the volume of this solid using geometry. However, there is another way to do so using calculus principles.

Disk Method

The volume of a solid is calculated by using the formula below.

$$V = \pi \int_a^b \left(f(x)\right)^2 dx$$

This method is called the disk method and is used for slices made perpendicular to the axis of revolution.

The term slice is used because of the method of calculating an integral. If you imagine taking a cross-section out of the cone, a circle of radius y would result. Now, if all of the cross sections of the cone were summed together, the entire volume of the cone would result. The integral is accomplishing this same process, taking an infinite number of cross sections and adding them all together to find the volume.

Notice how the disk method formula is very similar to the geometric formula for calculating the volume of the cone.

$$V = \frac{1}{3}\pi r^2 h$$

Notice how the $\frac{1}{3}$ and the h values are missing in the disk method formula. The fraction is accounted for by the varying height of the slices calculated by the integral, and the height is accounted for by the dx or the change in the variable used in the integral. This makes sense, as the total height of the cone would be 4, which is the change in x from 0 to the restricted value of 4. The volume of the cone using the disk method would result in the form below.

$$V = \pi \int_0^4 (x)^2 dx = \left[\frac{1}{3}\pi x^3\right]_0^4 = \frac{64}{3}\pi$$

This is the same as the result from calculating the volume geometrically.

What if we instead calculated the volume of the surface rotated around the y-axis? The same cone would result, however, the notation for disk method would change.

$$V = \pi \int_0^4 (y)^2 \, dy$$

Notice how the height is now a change in y represented by dy, and the function inside the integral is now in terms of y.

Although the limits are the same, they are technically values of y in this formula, rather than values of x.

Shell Method

All volumes can also be calculated using a different method.

Shell method uses the formula below but uses slices that are parallel to the axis of revolution.

$$V = 2\pi \int_a^b (f(x) \cdot h) \, dx$$

This formula is different from the shell method because the slices are no longer circles, but rather, are shells or circumferences of the solid.

If a perpendicular cut were made in a cone and revolved around the center of the solid, a circle would result. However, the distance cut around the solid is the circumference of the resulting circle cross section. If all of these circumferences were summed together and multiplied by the height, the volume of the solid would result.

Notice how the shell method formula is very similar to the formula for circumference of a circle, being $2\pi r$.

Going back to the original example, if $y = x$ was revolved around the y-axis, the volume of the solid from $0 \leq x \leq 4$ formed from revolving the function can be found by the integral on the following page.

$$V = 2\pi \int_0^4 x(4 - x)dx = \frac{64\pi}{3}$$

Notice how in this example, the radius is equal to the value of x, while the height, the value of $4 - y$, results due to the distance between the cone's base and the function value on $y = x$. Often, visualizing the graph can help in solving solids of revolution problems. The graph for the revolution of $y = x$ around the y-axis can be seen below.

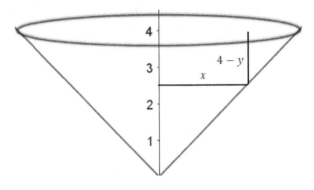

Volumes Between Curves

Volumes can also be found by the revolution of the region bounded between two curves. This is done using the formula below.

<u>Washer Method</u>

$$V = \pi \int_a^b \left(\left(f(x)\right)^2 - \left(g(x)\right)^2 \right) dx$$

Where $f(x)$ is the upper or outer curve and $g(x)$ is the lower or inner curve. You may notice that this formula is very similar to the formula for area between curves.

An easy way to remember this formula is to recognize that it is merely finding two separate volume curves and subtracting the inner curve's volume. Notice how both functions are squared, which shows that they both represent radii of different volumes. This principle will make more sense in the example below.

7.8 Find the volume of the solid formed by the revolution of the region bounded between the curves $y = x$ and $y = x^2$ around the x-axis.

To solve this problem, we must first identify which curve is the upper and which is the lower.

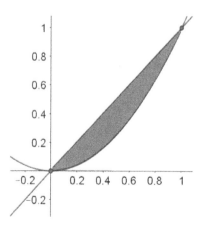

It can be seen that the curves intersect at the points $(0,0)$ and $(1,1)$. This can also be solved for algebraically. It can be observed that for the shaded region, $y = x$ is the upper curve while $y = x^2$ is the lower curve, as the solid is being revolved around the x-axis. The volume is then calculated using the formula as seen below.

$$V = \pi \int_0^1 ((x)^2 - (x^2)^2)dx = \frac{2\pi}{15}$$

The integral must be taken with respect to x, as the change in x represents the change in height as the integral calculates the volume formed by the bounded region. Notice how the formula is very similar to the formula for the disk method, so similar principles must be used to identify the different parts of the integral. We can recognize the limits of the integral based on the fact that the integral is being taken with respect to x, so both the lower and upper limits will be the two values of x that bound the region.

Volumes of Known Cross Sections

The use of the integral to calculate volumes of solids can be done for solids other than those created by revolved functions.

The basic formula for the volume of known cross sections is of the form below.

$$\int_a^b A(c)dc$$

Where $A(c)$ is the area of the known cross section with respect to variable c, which will be either x or y.

7.9 $y = -(x - 2)^2 + 4 \quad 0 \leq x, 0 \leq y$

Look at the graph of the function, restricted to the first quadrant.

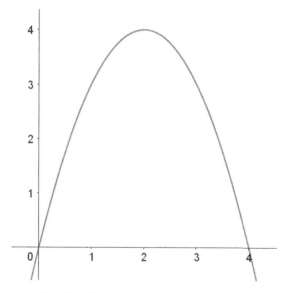

Now imagine that this function was the outline of a solid, 3-dimmensional shape. What shape would it form? It depends on the cross-section, or shape that is formed if the solid were to be cut.

Let's identify the volume of the solid using the function if it's vertical cross sections were squares. Just like how sequential cross section areas were summed together using shell of disk method, the same principle is used to calculate volumes of known cross sections.

First, the formula for the area of each cross section must be identified. The area of a square is base times height or s^2, since all the sides are equal in length. Since the function is restricted by the x and y axes, the length of each square cross section will be equal to the distance between the x-axis and the function, which is equivalent to y. This means that the area of each square cross section will be y^2. However, since the cross sections are vertical, being perpendicular to the x-axis, the thickness of each cross section is not a change in y, but rather a change in x, which means the integral will need to be in terms of x.

$$V = \int_0^4 (-(x-2)^2 + 4)^2 dx = \frac{512}{15}$$

The limits of the graph were obtained by observing where the graph intersects the x-axis. These limits could also be solved for algebraically. The volume results in the form above.

It is important to remember basic geometry to calculate the area of a wide variety of cross sections.

On the following page there is a table of useful geometric areas to put to memory. These will help in solving volume of known cross section problems.

Geometric Areas	
Triangle	$A = \dfrac{1}{2} b \cdot h$
Trapezoid	$A = \dfrac{1}{2}(b_1 + b_2)h$
Circle	$A = \pi r^2$
Rectangle	$A = b \cdot h$
Regular Polygon (Includes shapes such as pentagons, hexagons, and octagons)	$A = \dfrac{1}{2} \cdot a \cdot p$

*b is the base, h is the height, r is the radius, a is the apothem, and p is the perimeter.

Practice problems for this chapter can be found starting on the following page.

Chapter 7 Practice Problems

Eliminate the parameter in each of the following

1. $x = \sec(t), \quad y = \tan(t)$

2. $x = t^2, \quad y = t + 3$

3. $x = 4e^t, \quad y = t$

4. $x = \sin(t), \quad y = t^3$

5. $x = t^{\frac{1}{3}}, \quad y = \cos(t)$

Find $\frac{dy}{dx}$ and $\frac{dy^2}{d^2x}$ for each of the following. Leave in terms of t.

6. $x = \sin(t), \quad y = t$

7. $x = t^3 + 4, \quad y = \cos(3t)$

8. $x = \cos(t), \quad y = e^t$

9. $x = 4t^2, \quad y = t$

10. $x = \ln(t), \quad y = t^3$

For the previous 5 questions, replace t with terms of y and x. Also identify points of horizontal tangency.

For each of the following, identify the position function and acceleration function.

11. $v(t) = 4t^2 + \ln(t)$

12. $v(t) = \cos(3t)$

13. $v(t) = e^{3t} + 6$

14. $v(t) = t \cdot \ln(t^2)$

15. $v(t) = \sin(t) \cdot e^{\cos(t)}$

Identify the length of the curve represented by the parametric equations for each of the following. Use a calculator when necessary.

16. $x = t^2 + 3, \quad y = t^3, \quad 3 \le x \le 12$

17. $x = 2t, \quad y = e^t, \quad 3 \le t \le 4$

For each of the following, identify the total distance and the displacement of the particle given by the position function over the time given.

18. $s(t) = \cos(t), \quad 0 \le t \le \frac{\pi}{2}$

19. $s(t) = \ln(3t) + 1, \quad 2 \le t \le 6$

20. $s(t) = t^3 + 6t, \quad \frac{1}{2} \le t \le 10$

21. $s(t) = e^{6t}, \quad 0 \le t \le 3$

22. $s(t) = 10t^2, \quad 2 \le t \le 7$

For each of the following, identify the speed of the particle at the given time.

23. $s(t) = 4t^2, \quad t = 4$

24. $s(t) = \ln(2t), \quad t = \frac{1}{2}$

25. $s(t) = \cos(3t^2), \quad t = \sqrt{\pi}$

Solve each of the following related rate problems.

26. Find the rate of change of the length of a 5-foot-tall boy's 4 foot long shadow as he walks away from a 10-foot light pole at a rate of 6 feet per second.

27. What is the rate of change of the distance between a biker traveling on the ground at a rate of 6 feet per second and a balloon, which travels vertically off the ground at a rate of 10 feet per second, when the balloon is 5 feet off the ground? The balloon and the biker both leave from the same starting position at the same time.

28. A 12-foot ladder slides down a wall at a rate of 2 feet per second. At what rate is the foot of the ladder sliding away from the base of the wall when the ladder is 4 feet off the ground?

29. A semi-spherical pool is being filled with water at a rate of $24 \text{ cm}^3 \text{ } s^{-1}$. At what rate is the radius of the volume of water in the pool changing when the radius is 4 cm long?

30. A bag of sand pours out on the ground in a conical pile at a rate of 12 cm^3 per second. At what rate does the height of cone change when the radius is 2 cm? Assume that the height of the cone is equal to the radius.

31. A balloon fills with air at a rate of $4 \text{ ft}^3 \text{ min}^{-1}$. As it expands, the balloon forms a sphere. At what rate is the surface area of balloon changing when its radius is 6 inches.

32. A boy 12 meters away watches a bottle rocket launch vertically off the ground at a rate of 10 meters per second. At what rate is the angle of elevation between the boy and the rocket changing when the rocket is 20 meters off the ground.

33. Find the rate of movement of the tip of a 4-foot girl's 2 foot shadow when she walks away from a 10-foot light pole at a rate of 4 feet per second.

Find the volume of the solid formed by the revolution of each of the following functions around the given axis. Use a calculator when necessary.

34. $y = x^2$ around the x-axis, $0 \leq x \leq 3$

35. $y = \ln(x^2)$ around the y-axis, $1 \leq x \leq 2$

36. $y = e^x$ around $y = 2$, $1 \leq x \leq 3$

37. $y = \cos(2x)\, e^{\sin(2x)}$ around x-axis, $0 \leq x \leq \pi$

For each of the following, identify the volume formed by the revolution of the region bounded by the two given curves around the given axis.

38. $y = x^3$ and $y = x^2$ around the x-axis.

39. $y = \sin(x)$ and $y = \cos(x)$ around x-axis. $0 \le x \le \frac{\pi}{4}$

40. $y = x + 2$ and $y = x^2$ around the x-axis.

41. $y = e^x$ and $y = e^{2x}$ around y-axis. $1 \le y \le e$

Hint: Use a calculator to solve 41.

Identify the integral necessary to calculate the volume formed by the revolution of the curve made up of the given cross section. Do not evaluate the integral. Assume all cross sections are bounded by the curve and the x-axis.

42. $y = x^2$ with square cross sections. $0 \le x \le 4$

43. $y = \sin(5x)$ with equilateral triangle cross sections. The length of one side is equal to the height of the function.

$0 \le x \le \frac{\pi}{5}$

44. $y = e^x$ with semi-circular cross sections. $-1 \le x \le 1$

45. $y = \ln(x)$ with hexagonal cross sections, where the height of the hexagon, or the distance between each opposite pair of bases, is the function value. $1 \le x \le 4$

Chapter 7 Practice Problem Answers

1. a $x^2 - y^2 = 1$

2. a $x = y^2 - 6y + 9$

3. a $y = \ln\left(\dfrac{x}{4}\right)$

4. a $x = \sin\left(y^{\frac{1}{3}}\right)$

5. a $y = \cos(x^3)$

6. a $\dfrac{dy}{dx} = \sec(t)$

$\dfrac{dy^2}{d^2x} = \sec^2(t)\tan(t)$

6. b $\dfrac{dy}{dx} = \sec(y)$

$\dfrac{dy^2}{d^2x} = \sec^2(y)\tan(y) = \dfrac{x}{\cos^3(y)}$

Horizontal Tangents: None

7. a $\dfrac{dy}{dx} = \dfrac{(-\sin(3t))}{t^2}$

$\dfrac{dy^2}{d^2x} = \dfrac{-3t \cdot \cos(3t) + 2\sin(3t)}{3t^5}$

7. b $\dfrac{dy}{dx} = -\dfrac{\sin\left(3(x-4)^{\frac{1}{3}}\right)}{3(x-4)^{\frac{2}{3}}}$

$\dfrac{dy^2}{d^2x} = \dfrac{\left(-(x-4)^{\frac{1}{3}}y + 2\sin\left((x-4)^{\frac{1}{3}}\right)\right)}{(x-4)^{\frac{5}{3}}}$

Horizontal Tangents: $t = \dfrac{\pi k}{3}, x = \left(\dfrac{\pi k}{3}\right)^3 + 4, t \neq 0$

---

8. a $\dfrac{dy}{dx} = \dfrac{e^t}{-\sin(t)}$

$\dfrac{dy^2}{d^2x} = \dfrac{-\sin(t) \cdot e^t - \cos(t) \cdot e^t}{-\sin^3(t)}$

8. b $\dfrac{dy}{dx} = \dfrac{y}{-\sin(\ln(y))}$

$\dfrac{dy^2}{d^2x} = \dfrac{-\sin(\ln(y))\, y - xy}{-\sin^3(\ln(y))}$

Horizontal Tangents: None

9. a $\dfrac{dy}{dx} = \dfrac{1}{8t}$

$\dfrac{dy^2}{d^2x} = -\dfrac{1}{64t^3}$

9. b $\dfrac{dy}{dx} = \dfrac{1}{8y}$

$\dfrac{dy^2}{d^2x} = -\dfrac{1}{16xy}$

Horizontal Tangents: None

10. a $\dfrac{dy}{dx} = 3t^3$

$\dfrac{dy^2}{d^2x} = 9t^3$

10. b $\dfrac{dy}{dx} = 3y$

$\dfrac{dy^2}{d^2x} = 9y$

Horizontal Tangents: $t = 0, y = 0$

11. a $s(t) = \dfrac{4}{3}t^3 + t \cdot \ln(t) - t + s_0$

$a(t) = 8t + \dfrac{1}{t}$

12. a $s(t) = \dfrac{1}{3}\sin(3t) + s_0$

$a(t) = -3\sin(3t)$

13. a $s(t) = \dfrac{1}{3}e^{3t} + 6t + s_0$

$a(t) = 3e^{3t}$

14. a $s(t) = \dfrac{1}{2}t^2 \cdot \ln(t^2) - \dfrac{1}{2}t^2 + s_0$

$a(t) = 2 + \ln(t^2)$

15. a $s(t) = -e^{\cos(t)} + s_0$

$a(t) = -\sin^2(t) \cdot e^{\cos(t)} + \cos(t) \cdot e^{\cos(t)}$

16. a $\left[\dfrac{1}{27}(9t^2 + 4)^{\frac{3}{2}} \right]_0^3 = 28.728$

17. a 34.575

18. a Displacement $= -1$

Total Distance $= 1$

19. a Displacement = Total Distance $= \ln(6) - \ln(2)$

20. a Displacement = Total Distance $= 1056.875 = \dfrac{8455}{8}$

21. a Displacement = Total Distance $= e^{18} - 1$

22. a Displacement = Total Distance $= 450$

23. a 32

24. a 2

25. *a* 0

26. *a* 6 feet per second

27. *a* $\dfrac{68}{\sqrt{34}}$ feet per second

28. *a* $\dfrac{8}{\sqrt{128}}$ feet per second

29. *a* $\dfrac{3}{4\pi}$ cm s^{-1}

30. *a* $\dfrac{3}{\pi}$ cm s^{-1}

31. *a* 16 ft^2 min^{-1}

32. *a* $\dfrac{15}{68} \approx 0.2206$ radians per second

33. *a* $\dfrac{20}{3}$ ft s^{-1}

34. *a* $V = \pi \displaystyle\int_0^3 (x^2)^2 dx = \dfrac{243\pi}{5}$

35. *a* $V = 2\pi \displaystyle\int_1^2 (2-x)(\ln(x^2))dx = 0.545\pi$

36. *a* $V = \pi \displaystyle\int_1^3 (e^x - 2)^2 dx = 136.55\pi$

37. *a* $V = \pi \displaystyle\int_0^\pi \left(\cos(2x)\,e^{\sin(2x)}\right)^2 dx = 2.4986\pi$

38. *a* $V = \pi \displaystyle\int_0^1 ((x^2)^2 - (x^3)^2)dx = \dfrac{2\pi}{35}$

39. *a* $V = \pi \displaystyle\int_0^{\frac{\pi}{4}} ((\cos(x))^2 - (\sin(x))^2)dx = \dfrac{\pi}{2}$

40. a $V = \pi \int_{-1}^{2} ((x+2)^2 - (x^2)^2)dx = \dfrac{72\pi}{5}$

41. a $V = \pi \int_{0}^{e} \left((\ln(y))^2 - \left(\dfrac{1}{2}\ln(y) \right)^2 \right) dy = 2.0387\pi$

42. a $V = \int_{0}^{4} (x^2)^2 dx$

43. a $V = \int_{0}^{\frac{\pi}{5}} \left(\dfrac{\sqrt{3}}{4} \right) (\sin(5x))^2 dx$

44. a $V = \int_{-1}^{1} \dfrac{\pi}{2}(e^x)^2 \, dx$

45. a $V = \int_{1}^{4} \left(\dfrac{1}{2} \right) \left(\dfrac{1}{2}(\ln(x)) \right) \left(\dfrac{12\ln(x)}{\sqrt{3}} \right) dx$

Chapter 8: Polar Functions

Polar Form, Polar Derivatives, Integration in Polar Form, and Applications of Polar Integrals

Polar Form

Thus far we have only identified calculus principles on the xy or Cartesian plane. However, the polar form is another useful area where calculus principles can be applied to solve problems.

First, a quick review of polar form and coordinates.

Complex Number Plane

Polar form is used to identify complex numbers or numbers with an imaginary axis. In rectangular form, these complex numbers are identified in the form $a + bi$, where i is $\sqrt{-1}$.

In polar form, complex numbers are described by the form below.

$$z = r(\cos(\theta) + i\sin(\theta))$$

This form is sometimes abbreviated in the form below.

$$r\text{cis}(\theta)$$

Either way, they are both describing the same complex number plane.

The conversion between rectangular and polar coordinates is done by using the equations below.

$$r = |z| = \sqrt{a^2 + b^2}$$

$$a = r \cdot \cos(\theta)$$

$$b = r \cdot \sin(\theta)$$

$$\theta = \tan^{-1}\left(\frac{b}{a}\right)$$

8.1 Convert the complex number $4 + 3i$ into polar form.

$$r = \sqrt{4^2 + 3^2} = \sqrt{25} = 5$$

$$\theta = \tan^{-1}\left(\frac{3}{4}\right) \approx 0.644$$

Be sure to always use radians when using trig functions in calculus. The derivative and integral tools do no work in the same way when degrees are used.

$$z = 5\big(\cos(0.644) + i(\sin(0.644))\big) = 5\text{cis}(0.644)$$

8.2 Convert the complex number $-7 + 7i$ to polar form.

$$r = \sqrt{49 + 49} = \sqrt{98} \approx 9.899$$

$$\theta \neq \tan^{-1}\left(\frac{7}{7}\right) = \tan^{-1}(1) = \frac{\pi}{4}$$

However, the angle is not truly $\frac{\pi}{4}$. Let's observe the graph for the complex number.

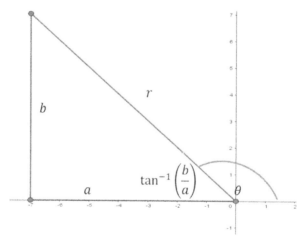

Notice that the angle for the polar coordinate always starts from the positive side of the real number axis and travels counter-clockwise. For this number, the inverse tangent does not calculate the angle needed for the polar coordinates. To find θ, we must subtract $\tan^{-1}\left(\frac{b}{a}\right)$ from π.

$$\theta = \pi - \tan^{-1}(1) = \frac{3\pi}{4}$$

It is often useful to draw the coordinates in the complex number plane for reference.

$$z = \sqrt{98}\,\text{cis}\left(\frac{3\pi}{4}\right)$$

Cartesian Plane

However, polar form is also used for traditional Cartesian graphing. Let's observe the graph of the circle below.

8. 3 $x^2 + y^2 = 4$

This is not in the complex number plane but is rather in the Cartesian plane.

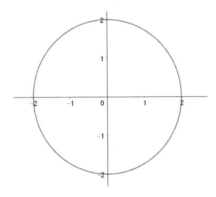

This is the graph for a circle centered at the origin with a radius of 2.

Let's substitute $r\cos(\theta)$ for x and $r\sin(\theta)$ for y in the equation.

r in this equation is 2, as the circle's radius is 2. However, we will observe that r is not always a constant and can be a function of θ, $f(\theta)$.

$$(2\cos(\theta))^2 + (2\sin(\theta))^2 = 4(\cos^2(\theta) + \sin^2(\theta)) = 4 = r^2$$

This proves that the value of r is 2 or -2, however, you may notice later how for polar coordinates in the Cartesian plane these values of r are equivalent.

This is the method used to convert Cartesian equations into polar form. Always use the substitutions below and isolate for r to convert Cartesian equations into polar form.

$$x = r\cos(\theta)$$

$$y = r\sin(\theta)$$

$$r = \sqrt{x^2 + y^2}$$

For a circle, the graph in polar form is merely of the form below.

$$r = a$$

Where a is a constant and is equal to the radius of the circle.

Graphing polar shapes are done by graphing every value of r from 0 to 2π. The angle values for a polar graph always start from the positive side of the x-axis and travel counterclockwise.

Polar graphs are always of the form $r = f(\theta)$. Here are some traditional shapes in polar form that may be helpful for principles later in this chapter.

Notice in the graphs on the next few pages how the limacon has a loop while the cardioid looks like a heart. Also notice how vertically oriented shapes use sine while horizontal shapes use cosine. These shapes and patterns will help when finding derivatives and integrals using polar graphs.

Polar Graphs	
Circle $$r = a$$	
Horizontal Cardioid $r = a \pm b\cos(\theta)$ Where $a \geq b$	

Vertical Cardioid $r = a \pm b\sin(\theta)$ Where $a \geq b$	
Horizontal Limacon $r = a \pm b\cos(\theta)$ Where $a < b$	
Vertical Limacon $r = a \pm b\sin(\theta)$ Where $a \leq b$	

Other important graphing patterns to recognize are those of the form below.

$$r = \sin(c\theta) \text{ or } r = \cos(c\theta)$$

These are rose graphs, which form a flower shape.

The constant c causes petals to form. The number of petals that form about the origin is based on the value of c.

When c is an even number, $2c$ petals form.

When c is an odd number, c petals form.

For example, the graph of $r = \sin(2\theta)$ can be seen below.

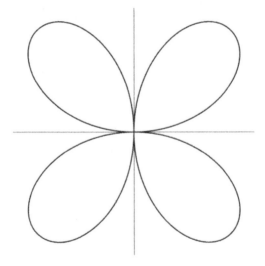

Notice how $2c$ or 4 petals formed. The length of the petals depends on the coefficient of the sine or cosine function, which was 1 in this case.

Derivation in Polar Form

The derivative principle can also be applied to polar graphs.

The derivative of a polar graph is of the form below.

$$\frac{dy}{dx} = \frac{\frac{dy}{d\theta}}{\frac{dx}{d\theta}} = \frac{\frac{d(r\sin(\theta))}{d\theta}}{\frac{d(r\cos(\theta))}{d\theta}}$$

Remember how when converting from Cartesian to polar form that x and y were replaced with $r\cos(\theta)$ and $r\sin(\theta)$ respectively. This will be used when deriving polar forms.

8.4 Find the derivative of $r = 4 + 4\cos(\theta)$.

Recognize the shape? While it is not necessary for this problem, the shape above is a horizontal cardioid.

To find the derivative, the polar form must be converted into Cartesian form.

$$x = (4 + 4\cos(\theta))(\cos(\theta)) = 4\cos(\theta) + 4\cos^2(\theta)$$

$$y = (4 + 4\cos(\theta))(\sin\theta) = 4\sin(\theta) + 4\sin(\theta)\cos(\theta)$$

$$\frac{dx}{d\theta} = -4\sin(\theta) - 8(\cos(\theta))(\sin(\theta))$$

$$\frac{dy}{d\theta} = 4\cos(\theta) + 4\cos^2(\theta) - 4\sin^2(\theta)$$

$$\frac{dy}{dx} = \frac{\frac{dy}{d\theta}}{\frac{dx}{d\theta}} = \frac{(4\cos(\theta) + 4\cos^2(\theta) - 4\sin^2(\theta))}{-4\sin(\theta) - 8(\cos(\theta))(\sin(\theta))}$$

Through simplifying by trig identities, we arrive at the form below.

$$\frac{dy}{dx} = \frac{(-\cos(\theta) - \cos(2\theta))}{\sin(\theta) + \sin(2\theta)}$$

8.5 This expression can then be used to identify the slope of the tangent line at the point (8,0) in (x, y).

First, the point in (x, y) must be converted to a point in polar form, (r, θ).

$$8 = 4\cos(\theta) + 4\cos^2(\theta)$$

$$0 = \cos^2(\theta) + \cos(\theta) - 2$$

$$0 = (\cos(\theta) + 2)(\cos(\theta) - 1)$$

$$\theta = \cos^{-1}(-2), 0$$

$$0 = 4\sin(\theta) + 4\sin(\theta)\cos(\theta)$$

$$0 = 4\sin(\theta)(1 + \cos(\theta))$$

$$\theta = 0, \pi$$

Solving for θ in both x and y ensures that there is only one correct value.

$$\theta = 0$$

After solving for θ, r can be determined by plugging that value into the r expression. $r = 4 + 4(\cos(0)) = 8$

The point in polar form is (8,0).

Now plug the value of θ into the derivative expression to find the slope of the tangent line at (8,0).

$$\frac{dy}{dx} \neq -\frac{2}{0} \therefore \text{Undefined/DNE}$$

This means that the derivative is undefined at the value. This can be clearly seen when the graph of the cardioid is visualized. This is why a proper knowledge of polar forms may come in handy.

Integration in Polar Form

Just as in rectangular form, integration can be used in polar graphing to identify the area underneath the curve.

Area Underneath Polar Curves

Use the formula below when finding the area underneath the curve for polar forms.

$$A = \frac{1}{2} \int r^2 d\theta$$

8. 6 Find the area under the curve for the polar equation

$$r = 3 + 2\sin(\theta).$$

This polar curve is a vertical cardioid. The limits for the area under the curve for this equation are 0 and 2π.

$$A = \frac{1}{2} \int_0^{2\pi} (3 + 2\sin(\theta))^2 d\theta$$

After using power reduction, the integral results in the form below.

$$\left[\frac{11}{2}\theta - 6\cos(\theta) - \frac{1}{2}\sin(2\theta) \right]_0^{2\pi} = 11\pi$$

8. 7 Find the area under the curve for the polar equation

$$r = 1 + 2\sin(\theta).$$

This curve is a vertical limacon, recall that this is the graph with a loop in it. We must be careful when calculating the area under the curve for this equation.

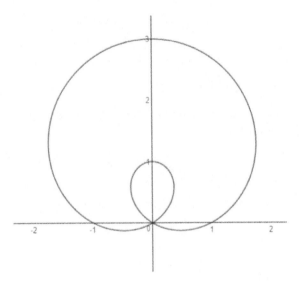

If we visualize the integral for the graph above and we simply used the limits 0 and 2π the area inside the loop would be counted twice. We must account for this when finding the area.

We must find where the equation begins to form the loop and ends the formation of the loop. Luckily, the radius is 0 at these values, as the loop forms about the origin.

$$0 = 1 + 2\sin(\theta)$$

$$\theta = \sin^{-1}\left(-\frac{1}{2}\right) = \frac{7\pi}{6}, \frac{11\pi}{6}$$

However, through using a calculator, only one value for the inverse sine would result. Be sure to include both values.

This means that our limits must be restricted based on the loop. We can use these limits to find the area under the curve in two ways.

First, we can find the area by subtracting the area in the loop so that it is only accounted for once in the area.

$$A = \frac{1}{2}\int_{0}^{2\pi}(1 + 2\sin(\theta))^2 d\theta - \frac{1}{2}\int_{\frac{7\pi}{6}}^{\frac{11\pi}{6}}(1 + 2\sin(\theta))^2 d\theta$$

$$A = \left[\frac{3}{2}\theta - 2\cos(\theta) - \frac{1}{2}\sin(2\theta)\right]_0^{2\pi}$$
$$- \left(\left[\frac{3}{2}\theta - 2\cos(\theta) - \frac{1}{2}\sin(2\theta)\right]_{\frac{7\pi}{6}}^{\frac{11\pi}{6}}\right)$$

$$A = 3\pi - \left(\pi - \frac{3\sqrt{3}}{2}\right) = 2\pi + \frac{3\sqrt{3}}{2}$$

The area can also be calculated by simply omitting the area in the loop.

$$A = \frac{1}{2}\int_0^{\frac{7\pi}{6}}(1 + 2\sin(\theta))^2\,d\theta + \frac{1}{2}\int_{\frac{11\pi}{6}}^{2\pi}(1 + 2\sin(\theta))^2\,d\theta$$

Notice how the beginning and end of the formation of the loop are the limits of the two separate integrals.

$$A = \left(\frac{7\pi}{4} + \frac{3\sqrt{3}}{4} + 2\right) + \left(\frac{\pi}{4} - 2 + \frac{3\sqrt{3}}{4}\right) = 2\pi + \frac{3\sqrt{3}}{2}$$

Notice how the same answer results using either method.

8. 8 Find the area underneath the curve below.

$r = 2\sin(3\theta)$

This is a rose graph with three petals. As there are no inner loops, the limits can be taken from 0 to 2π.

However, it may be beneficial to realize that each petal is symmetrical, which means that the area of one is equivalent to every other petal. This means that the area underneath the rose curve can be found in two different ways.

The petals each begin and end at $\frac{\pi k}{3}$, where k is any positive integer less than 7. This can be used to calculate the area more simply.

$$A = \frac{1}{2} \int_0^{2\pi} (2\sin(3\theta))^2 d\theta \text{ or } A = \frac{1}{2}(3) \int_0^{\frac{\pi}{3}} (2\sin(3\theta))^2 d\theta$$

$$A = 2\pi$$

Both result in the same answer, but in some cases, it may be easier to find the area of only a single petal.

Area Between Polar Curves

Use the formula below to find the area between two polar curves. You may notice that it is very similar to the formula for area between two Cartesian curves.

$$A = \frac{1}{2} \int \left((f_2(\theta))^2 - (f_1(\theta))^2 \right) d\theta$$

Where $f_2(\theta) = r_2$ is the outside polar form and $f_1(\theta) = r_1$ is the inside polar form. In polar form, outside and inside are considered rather than above and below as the functions surround one another in polar form while they do not in Cartesian forms.

8.9 Find the area between the two polar equations below.

$r = 3$

$r = 2 + \cos(\theta)$

We must first find where they intersect.

$$2 + \cos(\theta) = 3$$

$$\theta = 0$$

$r = 3$ is a circle, and $r = 2 + \cos(\theta)$ is a horizontal cardioid. It is also important to recognize that the circle of radius 3 is larger than the cardioid, so it is the outside function. Knowing this, we can find the area between the two curves.

$$A = \frac{1}{2} \int_0^{2\pi} ((3)^2 - (2 + \cos(\theta))^2) d\theta$$

As the curves only intersect at $\theta = 0$, the limits are from 0 to 2π.

$$A = \left[\frac{9}{4}\theta - 2\sin(\theta) - \frac{1}{8}\sin(2\theta)\right]_0^{2\pi} = \frac{9\pi}{2}$$

Arc Length of Polar Curves

You may also be asked to find the length of a polar curve between 2 restrictions. Use the formula below to find the arc length of polar curves.

$$L = \int_a^b \sqrt{r^2 + \left(\frac{dr}{d\theta}\right)^2}\, d\theta$$

8.10 Find the length of $r = 4 + \sin(\theta)$ from $0 \leq \theta \leq \frac{\pi}{2}$.

$$\frac{dr}{d\theta} = \cos(\theta)$$

$$L = \int_0^{\frac{\pi}{2}} \sqrt{(4 + \sin(\theta))^2 + \cos^2(\theta)}\, d\theta$$

It is unlikely that you will be asked to solve arc length integrals by hand, as the arc length integrals are often very difficult. In this case, we will just use the calculator.

$$L \approx 7.371$$

You can find practice problems for this chapter beginning on the next page.

<u>Chapter 8 Practice Problems</u>

Convert the following from Cartesian to polar form.

1. $x^2 + y^2 + 2y = 0$

2. $x^2 + y^2 = (x^2 - x + y^2)^2$

3. $x^2 + y^2 = (x^2 + y^2 - 2y)^2$

4. $x^2 + y^2 = \left(\frac{1}{4}\right)(x^2 + y^2 + 3y)^2$

5. $x^2 + y^2 = \left(\frac{1}{4}\right)^2 (x^2 + y^2 + y)^2$

Convert each of the following from polar to Cartesian form. Also identify the type of graph. Leave you answer in the form $x^2 + y^2 = z$.

6. $r = 2 + \sin(\theta)$

7. $r = 2 + 2\cos(\theta)$

8. $r = 2 - 3\sin(\theta)$

9. $r = 5$

10. $r = 3 + 5\cos(\theta)$

Find the slope of the tangent line at the given point for each of the following. Points are given in (r, θ).

11. $r = 3 + 2\sin(\theta)$, $\quad (3,0)$

12. $r = 5$, $\quad \left(5, \frac{\pi}{2}\right)$

13. $r = 2 - \sin(\theta)$, $\quad \left(1, \frac{\pi}{2}\right)$

14. $r = 2 + 5\cos(\theta)$, $\quad \left(4.5, \frac{\pi}{3}\right)$

15. $r = 1 + 2\sin(\theta)$, $\quad \left(2.732, \frac{\pi}{3}\right)$

16. $r = 1 - \sin(\theta)$, $\left(0.707, \frac{3\pi}{4}\right)$

17. $r = 3$, $\left(3, \frac{\pi}{4}\right)$

18. $r = 2 - 2\cos(\theta)$, $\left(3.732, \frac{5\pi}{6}\right)$

19. $r = 1 + 4\cos(\theta)$, $\left(3, \frac{5\pi}{3}\right)$

20. $r = 1 - 4\sin(\theta)$, $\left(-1, \frac{5\pi}{6}\right)$

Identify the area under the curve for each of the following. Use the constraints given. If no constraints are given, assume from 0 to 2π.

21. $r = 6$, $\quad 0 \leq \theta \leq \frac{\pi}{3}$

22. $r = 4 + 3\cos(\theta)$

23. $r = 2 + \cos(\theta)$

24. $r = 2 + 2\sin(\theta)$

25. $r = 3\sin(2\theta)$

26. $r = 2\cos(3\theta)$

27. $r = -\sqrt{2} + 2\cos(\theta)$

28. $r = -1 + 2\sin(\theta)$

29. $r = 3\sin(6\theta)$

30. $r = 4$, $\quad \frac{\pi}{4} \leq \theta \leq \frac{5\pi}{6}$

Identify the area between the two curves for each of the following.

31. $r = 4$

$r = 6$

32. $r = 3$

$r = 2\sin(3\theta)$

33. $r = 2$

$r = 1 + \cos(\theta)$

34. $r = 2$

$r = 1 + 2\sin(\theta)$

$$\frac{\pi}{6} \le \theta \le \frac{5\pi}{6}$$

35. $r = 2 + \cos(\theta)$

$r = \cos(3\theta)$

36. $r = 4$

$r = 4 + \cos(\theta)$

37. $r = 2$

$r = 2\cos(4\theta)$

38. $r = 1 + 2\cos(\theta)$

$r = 1$

(Hint: Use a calculator for 38)

Find the area of the inner loop of the following limacon

39. $r = -1 + 2\cos(\theta)$

Find the area of a single petal on the following rose

40. $r = 2\cos(6\theta)$

Find the arc length of the following on the given range. You may use a calculator.

41. $r = 1 + 2\cos(\theta)$, $0 \le \theta \le \frac{\pi}{2}$

42. $r = 4\cos(3\theta)$, $0 \le \theta \le \pi$

43. $r = 3 - 2\sin(\theta), \quad \frac{\pi}{2} \leq \theta \leq \pi$

44. $r = 2, \quad \frac{\pi}{3} \leq \theta \leq \frac{\pi}{2}$

45. $r = 1 + \sin(\theta), \quad 0 \leq \theta \leq \frac{3\pi}{2}$

Chapter 8 Practice Problem Answers

1. a $r = -2\sin(\theta)$

2. a $r = 1 + \cos(\theta)$

3. a $r = 1 + 2\sin(\theta)$

4. a $r = 2 - 3\sin(\theta)$

5. a $r = 4 - \sin(\theta)$

6. a $\frac{1}{4}(x^2 + y^2 - y)^2 = x^2 + y^2$

Vertical Cardioid

7. a $\frac{1}{4}(x^2 - 2x + y^2)^2 = x^2 + y^2$

Horizontal Cardioid

8. a $x^2 + y^2 = \frac{1}{4}(x^2 + y^2 + 3y)^2$

Vertical Limacon

9. a $x^2 + y^2 = 25$

Circle of radius 5

10. a $x^2 + y^2 = \frac{1}{9}(x^2 + y^2 - 5x)^2$

Horizontal Limacon

11. a $\frac{3}{2}$

12. a 0

13. a 0

14. a $\frac{\sqrt{3}}{7}$

15. $a \dfrac{1 + 2\sqrt{3}}{-2 - \sqrt{3}}$

16. $a \ 1 - \dfrac{\sqrt{2}}{2}$

17. $a - 1$

18. $a \ 1$

19. $a \dfrac{\left(4 + \sqrt{3}\right)}{2 + 4\sqrt{3}}$

20. $a - \dfrac{3\sqrt{3}}{5}$

21. $a \ A = 6\pi$

22. $a \ A = \dfrac{41}{2}\pi$

23. $a \ A = \dfrac{9\pi}{2}$

24. $a \ A = 6\pi$

25. $a \ A = \dfrac{9\pi}{2}$

26. $a \ A = 2\pi$

27. $a \ A = \ 3\pi + 3$

28. $a \ A = \ 2\pi + \dfrac{3\sqrt{3}}{2}$

29. $a \ A = \dfrac{9\pi}{2}$

30. $a \ A = \dfrac{14}{3}\pi$

31. $a \ 20\pi$

32. *a* 7π

33. *a* π

34. *a* $\dfrac{\sqrt{3}}{2} - \dfrac{\pi}{3} + 4$

35. *a* 4π

36. *a* 43.051

37. *a* 2π

38. *a* 1.196

39. *a* $\pi - \dfrac{3\sqrt{3}}{2}$

40. *a* $\dfrac{\pi}{6}$

41. *a* 4.300

42. *a* 26.730

43. *a* 3.399

44. *a* $\dfrac{\pi}{3}$

45. *a* 6.828

Chapter 9: Introduction to Series

Properties of Series, Taylor Series, Error Bounds, Tests for Convergence: n-th Term Test, p-series Test, Ratio Test, Direct Comparison Test, Limit Comparison Test, Integral Test, Alternating Series Test, and Radius and Interval of Convergence

Properties of Series

A sequence is a list of numbers that follow a certain pattern. An arithmetic sequence consists of consecutive numbers with a common difference, while a geometric sequence consists of consecutive numbers with a common multiplicative ratio. Examples of sequences are shown below.

Arithmetic: $2, 4, 6, 8, 10, 12, 14, 16$

Geometric: $2, 4, 8, 16, 32, 64, 128, 256, 512$

A series is a sum of the terms in a given sequence. The sequences above written as series are seen in the form below.

$$2 + 4 + 6 + 8 + 10 + 12 + 14 + 16$$

$$2 + 4 + 8 + 16 + 32 + 64 + 128 + 256 + 512$$

An infinite series of numbers is the sum of the terms of a sequence without a given final value. In sigma notation, the sum of an infinite series is of the form shown below.

$$S_\infty = \sum_{n=1}^{\infty} a_n$$

An infinite series converges if the partial sum approaches a fixed value (L) as more terms are added. This concept is represented in sigma notation below.

$$\sum_{n=1}^{\infty} a_n = L$$

An infinite series diverges if the partial sum does not approach a fixed value as more terms are added. This can be represented in sigma notation as shown below.

$$\sum_{n=1}^{\infty} a_n = \infty \therefore \text{Divergent}$$

The table below shows some of the basic formulas involving arithmetic and geometric series.

Basic Series Formulas	
Arithmetic Series Sum $a + (a + d) + (a + 2d) + \cdots + (a + (n - 1)d)$	$S_n = \dfrac{n}{2}[2a_1 + (n - 1)d]$
Geometric Series Partial Sum $a + ar + ar^2 + ar^3 + \cdots + ar^{n-1} = \displaystyle\sum_{n=1}^{\infty} ar^{n-1}$	$S_n = \dfrac{a(1 - r^n)}{1 - r}$
Convergent Infinite Geometric Series A geometric series can be identified as convergent if $\lvert r \rvert < 1$.	$S_\infty = \dfrac{a}{1 - r}$
p-series	$\displaystyle\sum_{n=1}^{\infty} \dfrac{1}{n^p}$
Divergent Harmonic Series	$\displaystyle\sum_{n=1}^{\infty} \dfrac{1}{n}$

9.1 Evaluate $1 + 3 + 5 + 7 + 9 + 11 + \cdots + 99$

This arithmetic series can be rewritten in the form shown below.

$$1 + (1 + 2) + (1 + 4) + (1 + 6) + \cdots + (1 + 98)$$

There are a total of 50 terms in the sequence, and $a_1 = 1, d = 2$

$$S_{50} = \frac{50}{2}[2 + (49 \cdot 2)]$$

$$S_{50} = 2500$$

9.2 Evaluate $2 + 4 + 8 + 16 + 32 + 64 \ldots 1024$

There are 10 terms in this geometric series, with $a = 2$ and $r = 2$. The geometric series partial sum is shown below.

$$S_{10} = \frac{2(1 - 2^{10})}{1 - 2} = 2046$$

9.3 Evaluate $\sum_{n=1}^{\infty} 4 \cdot \left(\frac{1}{2}\right)^n$

This series can be rewritten in the form below.

$$\sum_{n=1}^{\infty} 2 \cdot \left(\frac{1}{2}\right)^{n-1}$$

Since $r < 1$, the formula for the sum of the infinite geometric series can be used with the first term equal to 2.

$$S_{\infty} = \frac{2}{1 - \frac{1}{2}} = 4$$

Taylor Series

In order to estimate values on a given curve, a Taylor polynomial can be used to determine information about the curve at the point $x = a$. The polynomial allows for the representation of a function as an infinite series based on the function's derivative. A Taylor polynomial is a partial sum of a Taylor series. The basic Taylor series $P(x)$ is given by the formula below.

$$P(x) = f(a) + f'(a)(x - a) + \frac{f''(a)}{2!}(x - a)^2$$
$$+ \frac{f'''(a)}{3!}(x - a)^3 + \cdots + \frac{f^{(n)}(a)}{n!}(x - a)^n$$

A special case of the Taylor Series arises when the polynomial is centered at $x = 0$. This is known as the Maclaurin Series.

$$P(x) = f(0) + f'(0)x + \frac{f''(0)}{2!}x^2 + \cdots + \frac{f^{(n)}(0)}{n!}x^n$$

9.4 Find the Taylor Series $for\ f(x) = e^x$ centered at $x = 0$.

The derivatives of e^x are shown below.

$$f(x) = e^x$$
$$f'(x) = e^x$$
$$f''(x) = e^x$$
$$f'''(x) = e^x$$
$$f^{(n)}(x) = e^x$$

The Taylor Series can therefore be written in the form below.

$$P(x) = e^0 + e^0 x + \frac{e^0}{2!}x^2 + \cdots + \frac{e^0}{n!}x^n$$

Expressed in sigma notation, the Taylor series for e^x is seen below.

$$\sum_{n=0}^{\infty} \frac{x^n}{n!}$$

9.5 Find the Taylor series for $f(x) = e^x$ centered at $x = 1$.

Using the derivatives of e^x found in example 11.4, the Taylor polynomial can be expressed in the form below.

$$P(x) = e^1 + e^1(x-1) + \frac{e^1}{2!}(x-1)^2 + \cdots + \frac{e^1}{n!}(x-1)^n$$

9.6 Find the Maclaurin series for $f(x) = \sin(x)$.

Since this is a Maclaurin series, the function is centered at $x = 0$. The derivatives of $\sin(x)$ are as follows.

$$\begin{aligned}
f(x) &= \sin(x) \\
f'(x) &= \cos(x) \\
f''(x) &= -\sin(x) \\
f'''(x) &= -\cos(x) \\
f^{(4)}(x) &= \sin(x)
\end{aligned}$$

Evaluated at $x = 0$, the derivatives above result in the forms below.

$$\begin{aligned}
f(0) &= 0 \\
f'(0) &= 1 \\
f''(0) &= 0 \\
f'''(0) &= -1 \\
f^{(4)}(0) &= 0
\end{aligned}$$

Therefore, the series can be written in the following form.

$$P(x) = 0 + \frac{1}{1!}x + \frac{0}{2!}x^2 - \frac{1}{3!}x^3 + \frac{0}{4!}x^4 \ldots$$

Written in sigma notation, the series is equal to the following.

$$\sum_{n=0}^{\infty}(-1)^n \left(\frac{x^{(2n+1)}}{(2n+1)!}\right)$$

9.7 Find the third degree Taylor polynomial for $f(x) = \ln(x)$ centered at $x = 5$.

The first few derivatives of $\ln(x)$ are as follows.

$$f(x) = \ln(x)$$

$$f'(x) = \frac{1}{x}$$

$$f''(x) = -\frac{1}{x^2}$$

$$f'''(x) = \frac{2}{x^3}$$

Evaluated at the point $x = 5$, the results are shown below.

$$f(5) = \ln(5)$$

$$f'(5) = \frac{1}{5}$$

$$f''(5) = -\frac{1}{25}$$

$$f'''(5) = \frac{2}{125}$$

Writing out the Taylor polynomial to the third degree results in the following forms.

$$P(x) = \ln(5) + \frac{1}{5}(x - 5) - \frac{\frac{1}{25}}{2!}(x - 5)^2 + \frac{\frac{2}{125}}{3!}(x - 5)^3$$

$$P(x) = \ln(5) + \frac{1}{5}(x-5) - \frac{1}{50}(x-5)^2 + \frac{2}{750}(x-5)^3$$

The table below shows some of the most frequently seen series.

Basic Power Series	
$\dfrac{1}{1-x}$	$1 + x + x^2 + x^3 + \cdots = \displaystyle\sum_{n=0}^{\infty} x^n$
e^x	$1 + \dfrac{x}{1!} + \dfrac{x^2}{2!} + \dfrac{x^3}{3!} + \cdots = \displaystyle\sum_{n=0}^{\infty} \dfrac{x^n}{n!}$
$\sin(x)$	$x - \dfrac{x^3}{3!} + \dfrac{x^5}{5!} - \dfrac{x^7}{7!} + \cdots = \displaystyle\sum_{n=0}^{\infty}(-1)^n \left(\dfrac{x^{(2n+1)}}{(2n+1)!} \right)$
$\cos(x)$	$1 - \dfrac{x^2}{2!} + \dfrac{x^4}{4!} - \dfrac{x^6}{6!} + \cdots = \displaystyle\sum_{n=0}^{\infty}(-1)^n \left(\dfrac{x^{2n}}{(2n)!} \right)$
$\arctan(x)$	$x - \dfrac{x^3}{3} + \dfrac{x^5}{5} - \dfrac{x^7}{7} + \cdots = \displaystyle\sum_{n=0}^{\infty}(-1)^n \left(\dfrac{x^n}{2n+1} \right)$
$\ln(1+x)$	$x - \dfrac{x^2}{2} + \dfrac{x^3}{3} - \dfrac{x^4}{4} + \cdots = \displaystyle\sum_{n=1}^{\infty} \dfrac{(-1)^{n-1}x^n}{n!}$
$(1+x)^k$	$1 + kx + \dfrac{k(k-1)}{2}x^2 + \dfrac{k(k-1)(k-2)}{3!}x^3 + \cdots = \displaystyle\sum_{n=0}^{\infty} \binom{k}{n} x^n$

Lagrange Error Bounds

A value on the function $f(x)$ can be estimated using the n-th degree Taylor polynomial $P_n(x)$. The error caused by the estimation of the Taylor polynomial is represented mathematically in the form below.

$$E_n(x) = f(x) - P_n(x)$$

Since the Taylor Polynomial can be an overestimate or an underestimate, the error function is written in the form below.

$$|E_n(x)| = |f(x) - P_n(x)|$$

The Lagrange Error bound for an n-th degree Taylor Polynomial, $P_n(x)$, is defined by the formula below.

$$|E_n(x)| \le \frac{\left|f^{(n+1)}(z)\right|}{(n+1)!}|x - a|^{(n+1)}$$

Where a is the center of the Taylor polynomial, n is the degree of the polynomial, and $f^{n+1}(z)$ is the maximum output value between x and a. The examples below will help clarify the method to calculating the Lagrange Error Bound for a Taylor Polynomial.

9.8 Find the error bound for the 3rd degree Maclaurin polynomial of $f(x) = e^x$ approximating e^1.

The third degree Taylor polynomial for e^1 is of the form below.

$$P_3(x) = 1 + \frac{(1)}{1!} + \frac{(1)^2}{2!} + \frac{(1)^3}{3!} = 2.667$$

Using the formula for the Lagrange error above, we find that the error is of the form shown below.

$$|E_3(x)| \le \frac{\left|f^{(4)}(z)\right|}{4!}x^4$$

The given value of a is 0, and the given value of x is 1. The z value can therefore be calculated by substituting 0 and 1 into e^x.

$$e^0 = 1, e^1 = e$$

Since the highest output occurs at e^1 on this interval, the corresponding value of z is 1.

$$|E_3(x)| \leq \frac{\left|f^{(4)}(1)\right|}{4!}(1)^4$$

$$|E_3(x)| \leq \frac{e^1}{4!}(1)^4$$

$$|E_3(x)| \leq 0.113$$

Therefore the maximum error bound for the calculated value of e^1 is equal to 0.113.

9.9 How many terms of the Taylor series for $f(x) = e^x$ centered at $x = 0$ are required to estimate e^1 with an error less than 0.01?

On the interval $[0,1]$, the highest value of e^x is e. Using the formula for the error bound, we arrive at the expression below.

$$\frac{e}{(n+1)!}(1-0)^{n+1} = \frac{e}{(n+1)!}$$

Since we want this error to be less than or equal to 0.01, we set the equation less than or equal to the desired error.

$$\frac{e}{(n+1)!} \leq 0.01$$

The best way to solve the equation above is to guess and check using a calculator. This gives $n = 5$. Therefore, 5 terms of the Taylor series are needed to calculate the value of e within 0.01.

Tests for Convergence of Series

The convergence or divergence of a series is the determination of the infiniteness or finiteness of a sum of terms. If a series of terms approaches a value and is finite, it is considered to be convergent. If a series of terms does not approach a value or tends towards infinity, it is considered divergent. The tests for convergence or divergence allow us to determine the behavior of a series based on its composition.

n-th Term Test

The n-th term test of divergence is mathematically represented in the form below.

$$\text{If } \lim_{n \to \infty} a_n \neq 0, \text{ then } \sum a_n \text{ diverges}$$

This series test cannot be used to prove convergence.

9.10 Determine if $\displaystyle\sum_{n=1}^{\infty} \frac{3n+1}{4n+4}$ converges or diverges using the n-th term test of divergence.

The limit as the series approaches is shown in the form below.

$$\lim_{n \to \infty} \frac{3n+1}{4n+4}$$

This results in a value of $\frac{3}{4}$. Since the limit as the series approaches infinity is not equal to 0, this series diverges.

9.11 Determine if $\displaystyle\sum_{n=1}^{\infty} \frac{1}{n}$ converges or diverges based on the n-th term test of divergence.

Using the n-th term test, the limit as $\frac{1}{n}$ approaches infinity is equal to zero. Although it may be tempting to state that this series converges due to the n-th term test, remember that this specific test only proves divergence. Therefore, we cannot determine if $\frac{1}{n}$ converges or diverges using the n-th term test.

p-Series Test

The general form for a *p*-series is shown below.

$$\sum_{n=1}^{\infty} \frac{1}{n^p} = \frac{1}{1^p} + \frac{1}{2^p} + \frac{1}{3^p} + \frac{1}{4^p} + \cdots$$

The p-series is convergent if and only if $p > 1$. If $p = 1$, the series is divergent. This special case, where $p = 1$, is known as the harmonic series.

$$\sum_{n=1}^{\infty} \frac{1}{n} = \frac{1}{1} + \frac{1}{2} + \frac{1}{3} + \frac{1}{4} + \cdots$$

9. 12 Determine if $\sum_{n=1}^{\infty} \frac{1}{n^2}$ diverges or converges.

This series can be identified as a *p*-series, with $p = 2$. Since $2 > 1$, we can conclude that this series is convergent.

9. 13 Determine if $\sum_{n=1}^{\infty} \frac{n^{26.125}}{n^{26.25}}$ diverges or converges.

Simplifying the series gives the following result.

$$\sum_{n=1}^{\infty} \frac{1}{n^{0.125}}$$

Since this is a *p*-series with $p < 1$, we can conclude that the series is divergent.

Ratio Test

The ratio test for series determines convergence or divergence based on the ratio between two consecutive terms in a series. This idea is mathematically represented in the form shown below.

$$\lim_{n \to \infty} \left| \frac{a_{n+1}}{a_n} \right| = L$$

If $L < 1$, the series converges.
If $L > 1$, the series diverges.
If $L = 1$, we cannot determine if the series converges or diverges and the ratio test fails.

9.12 Determine if $\displaystyle\sum_{n=1}^{\infty} \left(\frac{1}{3} \right)^n$ diverges or converges using the ratio test.

The a_{n+1} term is equal to $\left(\frac{1}{3} \right)^{n+1}$, and the a_n term is equal to $\left(\frac{1}{3} \right)^n$. Finding the limit of the ratio between these terms, we arrive at the form below.

$$\lim_{n \to \infty} \left| \frac{\left(\frac{1}{3} \right)^{n+1}}{\left(\frac{1}{3} \right)^n} \right|$$

$$\lim_{n \to \infty} \frac{3^n}{3^{n+1}} = \frac{1}{3}$$

Since the calculated value is less than 1, this series is convergent.

9.13 Determine if $\displaystyle\sum_{n=1}^{\infty} \frac{(n+1)!}{3^n}$ diverges or converges using the ratio test.

The a_{n+1} term is $\frac{(n+2)!}{3^{n+1}}$, and the a_n term is $\frac{(n+1)!}{3^n}$. Finding the limit of the ratio between these two terms results in the form below.

$$\lim_{n \to \infty} \left| \frac{\frac{(n+2)!}{3^{n+1}}}{\frac{(n+1)!}{3^n}} \right|$$

$$\lim_{n \to \infty} \frac{n+2}{3}$$

As n approaches infinity, so does $\frac{n+2}{3}$. This means that the series diverges by the ratio test.

Direct Comparison Test

The direct comparison test uses the idea of comparing two series to determine convergence or divergence. The parameters for the direct comparison test are shown below.

For series $\sum a_n$ and $\sum b_n$ with $0 \le a_n \le b_n$

1. If $\sum b_n$ converges then $\sum a_n$ also converges.

2. If $\sum a_n$ diverges then $\sum b_n$ also diverges.

9.14 Determine if $\sum_{n=1}^{\infty} \dfrac{1}{2+n^5}$ converges or diverges using the direct comparison test.

We are given the a_n series in this case, which is $\dfrac{1}{2+n^5}$. A related series with a greater value than a_n is $\dfrac{1}{n^5}$.

$$0 \le \frac{1}{2+n^5} \le \frac{1}{n^5}$$

After testing a few values for n in the inequality above, we can see that $\dfrac{1}{2+n^5}$ always has output values lower than $\dfrac{1}{n^5}$. The series $\dfrac{1}{n^5}$ converges since it is a p-series with $n > 1$. Since the greater series converges, so does the smaller series. Therefore $\sum_{n=1}^{\infty} \dfrac{1}{2+n^5}$ converges with a direct comparison to $\dfrac{1}{n^5}$.

9.15 Determine if $\sum_{n=1}^{\infty} \dfrac{1}{2n-1}$ converges or diverges using the direct comparison test.

The series in question can be compared to $\frac{1}{2n}$. We know that this series diverges, since it is a p-series with $n = 1$ (harmonic series). Additionally the values of $\frac{1}{2n-1}$ are always greater than the values of $\frac{1}{2n}$.

$$0 \leq \frac{1}{2n} \leq \frac{1}{2n - 1}$$

Since the lesser series diverges, the greater series diverges as well. Therefore, the series $\sum_{n=1}^{\infty} \frac{1}{2n-1}$ diverges with a direct comparison to $\frac{1}{2n}$.

Limit Comparison Test

The Limit Comparison Test uses the ratio between two related functions to determine convergence or divergence. The definition of the Limit Comparison Test is shown below.

For $\sum a_n$ and $\sum b_n$, with $a_n \geq 0$, and $b_n > 0$

$$\lim_{n \to \infty} \frac{a_n}{b_n} = c$$

If c is positive and finite, then both series either converge or diverge. The examples below show the method for determining the series a_n and b_n.

9.16 Determine if $\sum_{n=1}^{\infty} \frac{n^3}{(n+1)^4}$ converges or diverges using the limit comparison test.

It is given that a_n is equal to $\frac{n^3}{(n+1)^4}$. This expression is similar to the output values generated by this series is $\frac{1}{n}$, since the quotient of $\frac{n^3}{(n+1)^4}$ is close to $\frac{1}{n}$. The limit comparison is shown below.

$$\lim_{n \to \infty} \frac{\dfrac{n^3}{(n+1)^4}}{\dfrac{1}{n}} = 1$$

Since this limit is resulting in a positive finite value, we can determine that the series $\frac{n^3}{(n+1)^4}$ behaves in the same way as $\frac{1}{n}$. Since $\frac{1}{n}$ is a divergent harmonic series, $\frac{n^3}{(n+1)^4}$ is also a divergent series by limit comparison to $\frac{1}{n}$.

9.17 Determine if $\displaystyle\sum_{n=1}^{\infty} \frac{n^2}{(5n+3)^7}$ converges or diverges using the limit comparison test.

It is given that a_n is $\frac{n^2}{(5n+3)^7}$. This expression has similar outputs to the series $\frac{1}{n^5}$. The limit comparison can therefore be written in the form below.

$$\lim_{n\to\infty} \frac{\dfrac{n^2}{(5n+3)^7}}{\dfrac{1}{n^5}} = \frac{1}{5}$$

Since this limit is resulting in a positive finite value, we can determine that the series $\frac{n^2}{(5n+3)^7}$ behaves in the same way as $\frac{1}{n^5}$. Since $\frac{1}{n^5}$ is a convergent p-series, $\frac{n^3}{(n+1)^4}$ is also a convergent series with limit comparison to $\frac{1}{n^5}$.

Integral Test

The integral test for series calculates the area under the curve of the series to determine if the series is convergent or divergent. This is done using the process of improper integration. The parameters for the integral test are as follows.

For a function $f(x)$ that is positive, continuous, and decreasing on the interval $[k, \infty)$ with $f(n) = a_n$, the integral test shows the following.

1. If $\int_{k}^{\infty} f(x)\, dx$ is convergent, then $\sum_{n=k}^{\infty} a_n$ also converges.

2. If $\int_{k}^{\infty} f(x)\, dx$ is divergent, then $\sum_{n=k}^{\infty} a_n$ also diverges.

9. 18 Determine if $\sum_{n=1}^{\infty} \frac{1}{n}$ is convergent or divergent using the integral test.

In this case, the function $f(x) = \frac{1}{x}$. Integrating this improper integral gives the answer below.

$$\int_{1}^{\infty} \frac{1}{x}\, dx = [\ln|x|]_{k}^{\infty} = \lim_{b \to \infty} [\ln(b) - \ln(1)] = \infty$$

Since the improper integral evaluated is divergent, the series $\frac{1}{n}$ is divergent by the integral test.

9. 19 Determine if $\sum_{n=0}^{\infty} 4n^3 e^{-n^4}$ is convergent or divergent using the integral test.

The function $f(x) = 4x^3e^{-x^4}$. The improper integral of this function on the interval $[0, \infty)$ is as follows.

$$\int_0^\infty 4x^3e^{-x^4}$$

Using $u = -x^4$, $du = -4x^3 dx$, we arrive at the answer below.

$$\left[-e^{-x^4}\right]_0^\infty$$

$$\lim_{b \to \infty}\left[-e^{-b^4} - (-1)\right] = 0 + 1 = 1$$

Since this integral is equal to a finite value, the series converges by the integral test.

Alternating Series Test

The alternating series test for convergence is required for a series including the term $(-1)^n$ or $(-1)^{n+1}$. The parameters for the alternating series test are as follows.

For the series $\displaystyle\sum_{n=1}^{\infty}(-1)^n a_n$ or $\displaystyle\sum_{n=1}^{\infty}(-1)^{n+1} a_n$,

the alternating series identifies the following.

If $\displaystyle\lim_{n\to\infty}|a_n| = 0$ and $a_n > a_{n+1}$, then the alternating series converges.

There are certain cases in which the $(-1)^n$ term causes a divergent series to become convergent. For this type of series, the $(-1)^n$ term solely causes the series to converge. This is a conditionally convergent series.

Other series where the $(-1)^n$ term has no effect on the convergence of the series are called absolutely convergent. The series would be convergent even without the $(-1)^n$ term included in this case.

Additionally, the alternating series error is calculated by taking the absolute value of the next term in the series. The error value calculated allows us to determine the difference between the exact value of the series and the value of the partial sum being used in estimation.

9. 20 Determine if $\displaystyle\sum_{n=1}^{\infty} \frac{(-1)^{n+1}}{n}$ is convergent or divergent
and whether the series converges absoutely or conditionally.

This is an alternating series, as the $(-1)^{n+1}$ term is included in the numerator. In order to determine if the series is convergent, the limit as $\frac{1}{n}$ approaches infinity must be zero, and the terms must be decreasing.

$$\lim_{n\to\infty} \frac{1}{n} = 0 \text{ and} \frac{1}{n} > \frac{1}{n+1}$$

Therefore, this series converges. To determine if the series diverges conditionally or absolutely, remove the alternating term $(-1)^{n+1}$.

$$\sum \frac{1}{n}$$

This series, as we had previously determined by the integral test, is divergent. The inclusion of the alternating term has caused the series $\frac{(-1)^{n+1}}{n}$ to converge. Therefore, the series is conditionally convergent by the alternating series test.

9. 21 Determine if $\displaystyle\sum_{n=0}^{\infty} \frac{\sin\left(\frac{(2n-1)\pi}{2}\right)}{n^2}$ is convergent or
divergent and whether the series converges conditionally or absolutely.

Trying out some values for n in the numerator results in the following numbers.

$$n = 0 \to \sin\left(-\frac{\pi}{2}\right) = -1$$

$$n = 1 \to \sin\left(\frac{\pi}{2}\right) = 1$$

$$n = 2 \rightarrow \sin\left(\frac{3\pi}{2}\right) = -1$$

This pattern shows that the numerator can be replaced with the alternating term $(-1)^n$.

$$\sum_{n=0}^{\infty} \frac{(-1)^n}{n^2}$$

Using the alternating series test, we can conclude the following.

$$\lim_{n \to \infty} \frac{1}{n^2} = 0, \text{ and } \frac{1}{n^2} > \frac{1}{(n+1)^2}$$

Therefore the series converges by the alternating series test. Since the series $\frac{1}{n^2}$ would have converged without the alternating term included, this series converges absolutely.

9. 22 Determine the number of terms of the series $\displaystyle\sum_{n=1}^{\infty} \frac{(-1)^n}{n^2}$ that are required to have an error bound less than 0.001.

The $(n+1)^{th}$ term that has an absolute value less than 0.001 is calculated as follows.

$$\left|\frac{(-1)^{n+1}}{(n+1)^2}\right| \rightarrow \frac{1}{n^2 + 2n + 1} < 0.001$$

Solving for n in the inequality above, we find the inequality for n below.

$$n^2 + 2n + 1 > 1000$$

$$n \geq 31$$

This means that for the alternating series above with 31 terms or more, the error will be less than 0.001.

Radius and Interval of Convergence

The ratio test can be used to determine the radius and interval of convergence of a power series. This is done by finding the values of x for which the ratio between consecutive terms is less than 1. The interval of convergence includes all the values of x for which a power series converges. The radius of convergence is the number of values of x for which a power series converges. In mathematical notation, a power series converges for the values below.

$$|x - a| < R$$

Where a is the center of the power series and R is the radius of convergence for the series. The series diverges if $|x - a| > R$.

The interval of convergence is expressed in the form below.

$$a - R < x < a + R$$

Values not included in the interval above cause the series to diverge.

9.23 Determine the radius and interval of convergence for $\displaystyle\sum_{n=0}^{\infty} \frac{(n + 1)x^n}{3^n}$.

Begin by using the ratio test.

$$\lim_{n \to \infty} \left| \frac{(n + 2)x^{n+1}}{3^{n+1}} \cdot \frac{3^n}{(n + 1)x^n} \right|$$

$$\lim_{n \to \infty} \left| \frac{1}{3}x \cdot \frac{n + 2}{n + 1} \right|$$

Since the limit is in terms of n, the x term inside can be brought outside the limit.

$$\frac{1}{3}|x| \lim_{n \to \infty} \left| \frac{n+2}{n+1} \right|$$

The limit is equal to 1. Since we want the ratio between two consecutive terms to be less than 1, the following inequality is given below.

$$\frac{1}{3}|x| < 1$$

$$|x| < 3$$

The radius of convergence is equal to 3.

$$-3 < x < 3$$

The interval of convergence is $(-3,3)$. We must test the endpoints of the interval of convergence by substituting the values $x = -3$ and $x = 3$ into the given power series. This will ensure the values should not be included in the interval of convergence. Always test the endpoints of the interval of convergence, as they may behave differently depending upon the series given.

$$\sum_{n=0}^{\infty} \frac{(n+1)(-3)^n}{3^n} = \sum_{n=0}^{\infty} (-1)^n (n+1) \to \text{Divergent series}$$

$$\sum_{n=0}^{\infty} \frac{(n+1)(3)^n}{3^n} = \sum_{n=0}^{\infty} (n+1) \to \text{Divergent series}$$

Testing the endpoints shows that the values $x = -3$ and $x = 3$ cause the series to diverge, and therefore should not be included in the interval of convergence. This confirms the interval of convergence for the original series to be $(-3,3)$.

9.24 Determine the radius and interval of convergence for $\sum_{n=0}^{\infty} \dfrac{3^n(x+3)^n}{n+1}$.

Apply the ratio test to determine the possible x values for convergence.

$$\lim_{n\to\infty} \left| \frac{(x+3)^{n+1} \cdot 3^{n+1}}{n+2} \cdot \frac{n+1}{3^n \cdot (x+3)^n} \right|$$

This simplifies to the limit below.

$$\lim_{n\to\infty} \left| \frac{(x+3) \cdot 3 \cdot (n+1)}{(n+2)} \right|$$

The x function can be taken out of the limit as follows.

$$3|x+3| \lim_{n\to\infty} \left| \frac{n+1}{n+2} \right| < 1$$

$$3|x+3| < 1$$

$$|x+3| < \frac{1}{3}$$

The radius of convergence is equal to $\frac{1}{3}$.

Solving the absolute value function for the interval of convergence, we arrive at the inequality below.

$$-\frac{1}{3} < x+3 < \frac{1}{3}$$

$$-\frac{10}{3} < x < -\frac{8}{3}$$

Before confirming that this is the true interval of convergence for the series, we must test the endpoints of the calculated interval. This can be done by plugging in the two values in the inequality above into the original series as follows.

Testing $x = -\frac{10}{3}$

$$\sum_{n=0}^{\infty} \frac{3^n \left(-\frac{10}{3} + 3\right)^n}{n + 1} = \sum_{n=0}^{\infty} \frac{3^n \left(-\frac{1}{3}\right)^n}{n + 1} = \sum_{n=0}^{\infty} \frac{3^n (-1)^n}{(3^n)n + 1}$$

$$= \sum_{n=0}^{\infty} \frac{(-1)^n}{n + 1}$$

= Conditionally Convergent by Alternating Series Test

Testing $x = -\frac{8}{3}$

$$\sum_{n=0}^{\infty} \frac{3^n \left(-\frac{8}{3} + 3\right)^n}{n + 1} = \sum_{n=0}^{\infty} \frac{3^n (3^{-n})}{n + 1} = \sum_{n=0}^{\infty} \frac{1}{n + 1}$$

= Divergent by Limit Comparison

Therefore, the interval of convergence is of the form below.

$$-\frac{10}{3} \leq x < -\frac{8}{3}$$

You can find practice problems for this chapter beginning on the next page.

Chapter 9 Practice Problems

1. Find the 7th partial sum of $\sum_{n=1}^{\infty} 7(0.25)^n$.

2. Find the sum $\sum_{n=1}^{\infty} \frac{2^n}{3^{n+1}}$.

3. Find the sum $\sum_{n=2}^{\infty} \frac{4^n}{5^n}$.

4. Find the sum $\sum_{n=3}^{\infty} \frac{5^{n+1}}{7^n}$.

5. Find the 4th partial sum of $\sum_{n=1}^{\infty} \frac{e^2}{\pi^2} \left(\frac{3^n}{2^n} \right)$
(Use calculator if necessary).

6. Find the 3rd degree Taylor polynomial for $f(x) = x^2 e^x$ centered at $x = 0$.

7. Find the 2nd degree Taylor polynomial for $f(x) = 3x^2 + e^x$ centered at $x = 2$.

8. Find the 4th degree Taylor polynomial for $f(x) = \frac{7x}{(x+1)^2}$ centered at $x = 0$.

9. Find the 3rd degree Taylor polynomial for $f(x) = \sin(x)$ centered at $x = 1$.

10. Find the 4th degree Taylor polynomial for $f(x) = \cos(x) + \sin(x)$ centered at $x = \pi$.

11. Find the Taylor series for $f(x) = \dfrac{1}{1-x}$ centered at $x = 0$.

12. Find the 3rd degree Taylor polynomial for $f(x) = \dfrac{3x}{x^2 + 1}$ centered at $x = 0$.

13. Find the 3rd degree Taylor polynomial for $f(x) = e^x \sin(x)$ centered at $x = \pi$.

14. Find the 5th degree Taylor polynomial for $f(x) = \sin(x) \cos(x)$ centered at $x = 0$.

15. Find the 3rd degree Taylor polynomial for $f(x) = \tan(x)$ centered at $x = 0$.

16. Given the 5th degree Taylor series for $f(x) = \sin(x)$ centered at $x = 0$, what is the maximum error bound for the estimated value of $\sin(1)$?

17. Find the error bound for the 7th degree Maclaurin polynomial of $f(x) = e^x$ approximating e^1.

18. How many terms are required in the Maclaurin series expansion of $f(x) = \cos(x)$ to estimate $\cos(1)$ with a maximum error bound of 0.0001?

19. Determine the number of terms of the series $\displaystyle\sum_{n=1}^{\infty} \dfrac{(-1)^n}{n^2 - 3n + 1}$ that are required to have an error bound less than 0.0001.

20. Determine the number of terms of the series $\displaystyle\sum_{n=1}^{\infty} \dfrac{(-1)^n}{\ln(n)}$ that are required to have an error bound less than 0.1.

21. Determine if $\displaystyle\sum_{n=1}^{\infty} \frac{(n^2+1)}{(n+1)^2}$ converges or diverges using the n-th term test of divergence.

22. Determine if $\displaystyle\sum_{n=1}^{\infty} \frac{n^3+2n}{n^4+5n^3}$ converges or diverges using the n-th term test of divergence.

23. Determine if $\displaystyle\sum_{n=1}^{\infty} \frac{\cos(n)}{n^2}$ converges or diverges using the n-th term test of divergence.

24. Determine if $\displaystyle\sum_{n=1}^{\infty} \frac{3n+\cos(n)}{n^7}$ converges or diverges using the n-th term test of divergence.

25. Determine if $\displaystyle\sum_{n=1}^{\infty} \frac{(n^2+1)^3}{n^6}$ converges or diverges using the n-th term test of divergence.

26. Determine if $\displaystyle\sum_{n=1}^{\infty} \frac{(2n+1)!}{2^{(n-1)}}$ converges or diverges using the ratio test.

27. Determine if $\displaystyle\sum_{n=1}^{\infty} \frac{1^n}{3^{(n+1)}}$ converges or diverges using the ratio test.

28. Determine if $\displaystyle\sum_{n=1}^{\infty} \frac{n^2+3n}{2^n}$ converges or diverges using the ratio test.

29. Determine if $\displaystyle\sum_{n=1}^{\infty} \frac{n! \cdot 3^n}{4^n}$ converges or diverges using the ratio test.

30. Determine if $\displaystyle\sum_{n=1}^{\infty} \frac{(2n+1)!}{(n+1)!}$ converges or diverges using the ratio test.

31. Determine if $\displaystyle\sum_{n=1}^{\infty} \frac{1}{1+n^2}$ converges or diverges using the direct comparison test.

32. Determine if $\displaystyle\sum_{n=1}^{\infty} \frac{2}{3n^2-1}$ converges or diverges using the direct comparison test.

33. Determine if $\displaystyle\sum_{n=1}^{\infty} \frac{1}{2^n+n}$ converges or diverges using the direct comparison test.

34. Determine if $\displaystyle\sum_{n=1}^{\infty} \frac{n^4}{n^5+3}$ converges or diverges using the direct comparison test.

35. Determine if $\displaystyle\sum_{n=1}^{\infty} \frac{1}{n^6+n^4+6}$ converges or diverges using the direct comparison test .

36. Determine if $\displaystyle\sum_{n=1}^{\infty} \frac{n^4}{(n+1)^6}$ converges or diverges using the limit comparison test.

37. Determine if $\displaystyle\sum_{n=1}^{\infty} \frac{1}{3n^3 + 2n}$ converges or diverges using the limit comparison test.

38. Determine if $\displaystyle\sum_{n=1}^{\infty} \frac{2n^7}{4(n+1)^8}$ converges or diverges using the limit comparison test.

39. Determine if $\displaystyle\sum_{n=1}^{\infty} \frac{n^2}{(n+3)^3}$ converges or diverges using the limit comparison test.

40. Determine if $\displaystyle\sum_{n=1}^{\infty} \frac{(4n^2 + 3n)^2}{(n+3)^6}$ converges or diverges using the limit comparison test.

41. Determine if $\displaystyle\sum_{n=1}^{\infty} \frac{1}{1 + n^2}$ converges or diverges using the integral test.

42. Determine if $\displaystyle\sum_{n=1}^{\infty} ne^n$ converges or diverges using the integral test.

43. Determine if $\displaystyle\sum_{n=1}^{\infty} \sin(n)$ converges or diverges using the integral test.

44. Determine if $\displaystyle\sum_{n=1}^{\infty} \arctan(n)$ converges or diverges using the integral test.

45. Determine if $\displaystyle\sum_{n=1}^{\infty} \frac{1}{n^2 + 8n + 15}$ converges or diverges using the integral test.

46. Determine if $\displaystyle\sum_{n=1}^{\infty} \frac{(-1)^n}{(n+1)}$ converges or diverges using the alternating series test.

47. Determine if $\displaystyle\sum_{n=1}^{\infty} \frac{(-1)^{n+1} \cdot n^3}{n^3 + 6}$ converges or diverges using the alternating series test.

48. Determine if $\displaystyle\sum_{n=1}^{\infty} \frac{(-1)^n}{\sqrt[3]{n}}$ converges or diverges using the alternating series test.

49. Determine if $\displaystyle\sum_{n=1}^{\infty} \frac{(-1)^{n+4}}{4n^3 + 4n + 4}$ converges or diverges using the alternating series test.

50. Determine if $\displaystyle\sum_{n=1}^{\infty} \frac{\sin\left(\frac{\pi(2n-1)}{2}\right)}{n^2 + n}$ converges or diverges using the alternating series test.

51. Determine the radius and interval of convergence for
$$\sum_{n=1}^{\infty} \frac{(x+3)^n}{7^n}.$$

52. Determine the radius and interval of convergence for
$$\sum_{n=1}^{\infty} \frac{(5x-2)^n}{n^2}.$$

53. Determine the radius and interval of convergence for

$$\sum_{n=1}^{\infty} \frac{2^n}{4^n}(x+3)^n.$$

54. Determine the radius and interval of convergence for

$$\sum_{n=1}^{\infty} \frac{(-1)^n(x+5)^n}{n \cdot 7^n}.$$

55. Determine the radius and interval of convergence for

$$\sum_{n=1}^{\infty} \frac{(2n+2)!}{(2n+1)!} \cdot x^n.$$

Use any series test to prove Convergence or Divergence

56. $\sum_{n=1}^{\infty} \frac{1}{n \cdot \ln(n)}$

57. $\sum_{n-1}^{\infty} \frac{(n+1)!}{n \cdot 4^n}$

58. $\sum_{n=1}^{\infty} \frac{2}{(n^2+4)^3}$

59. $\sum_{n=1}^{\infty} \frac{n}{n^2+4}$

60. $\sum_{n=1}^{\infty} \frac{(-1)^n(n+3) \cdot 3^n}{5^n}$

61. $\sum_{n=1}^{\infty} \frac{1}{\sqrt{n^2-9}}$

62. $\displaystyle\sum_{n=1}^{\infty} \frac{\ln(n)}{n^4}$

63. $\displaystyle\sum_{n=1}^{\infty} \frac{\pi^2}{e^2} \cdot \frac{n^2}{n^3}$

64. $\displaystyle\sum_{n=1}^{\infty} \frac{n^{3.25}}{n^{3.5}}$

65. $\displaystyle\sum_{n=1}^{\infty} n\ln(n)$

66. $\displaystyle\sum_{n=1}^{\infty} \frac{(3n+1)!}{3^n - 1}$

67. $\displaystyle\sum_{n=1}^{\infty} n^5 e^{-n^6}$

68. $\displaystyle\sum_{n=1}^{\infty} \frac{7n!}{(n+3)^2}$

69. $\displaystyle\sum_{n=1}^{\infty} \frac{e^{-n}}{n!}$

70. $\displaystyle\sum_{n=1}^{\infty} \frac{n}{n^2 - 1}$

71. $\displaystyle\sum_{n=1}^{\infty} \frac{n^2 + n}{3^n}$

72. $\displaystyle\sum_{n=1}^{\infty} \frac{(-1)^n \cdot 3^n}{n^3 + 4}$

73. $\displaystyle\sum_{n=1}^{\infty} \frac{n^2}{(n^3 + 4n + 3)^2}$

74. $\displaystyle\sum_{n=1}^{\infty} \frac{(n + 1)^2}{(n - 1)!}$

75. $\displaystyle\sum_{n=1}^{\infty} \frac{(-1)^{n+3} \cdot (3)^{n+1}}{5^n}$

Chapter 9 Practice Problem Answers

1. *a* 2.333

2. *a* $\frac{2}{3}$

3. *a* 3.2 *or* $\frac{16}{5}$

4. *a* $\frac{625}{98}$

5. *a* 9.124

6. *a* $f(x) = x^2 + x^3$

7. *a* $f(x) = 12 + e^2 + (12 + e^2)(x - 2) + \frac{6+e^2}{2}(x - 2)^2$

8. *a* $f(x) = 7x - 14x^2 + 21x^3 - 28x^4$

9. *a* $f(x) = \sin(1) + \cos(1)(x - 1) - \frac{\sin(1)}{2}(x - 1)^2 - \frac{\cos(1)}{6}(x - 1)^3$

10. *a* $f(x) = -1 - (x - \pi) + \frac{1}{2}(x - \pi)^2 + \frac{1}{6}(x - \pi)^3 - \frac{1}{24}(x - \pi)^4$

11. *a* $f(x) = 1 + x + x^2 + x^3 \dots = \sum_{n=0}^{\infty} x^n$

12. *a* $f(x) = 3x - 3x^3$

13. *a* $f(x) = -e^\pi(x - \pi) - e^\pi(x - \pi)^2 - \frac{e^\pi}{3}(x - \pi)^3$

14. *a* $f(x) = x - \frac{2}{3}x^3 + \frac{2}{15}x^5$

15. *a* $f(x) = x + \frac{1}{3}x^3$

16. *a* 0.00117

17. *a* 0.0000674

18. *a* 7 terms

19. *a* 101 terms

20. *a* 22026 terms

21. *a* Diverges

22. *a* Cannot determine using n-th term test

23. *a* Cannot determine using n-th term test

24. *a* Cannot determine using n-th term test

25. *a* Diverges

26. *a* Diverges

27. *a* Converges

28. *a* Converges

29. *a* Diverges

30. *a* Diverges

31. *a* Converges

32. *a* Converges

33. *a* Converges

34. *a* Diverges

35. *a* Converges

36. *a* Converges

37. *a* Converges

38. *a* Diverges

39. *a* Diverges

40. *a* Converges

41. *a* Converges

42. *a* Diverges

43. *a* Diverges

44. *a* Diverges

45. *a* Converges

46. *a* Converges Conditionally

47. *a* Diverges

48. *a* Converges Conditionally

49. *a* Converges Absolutely

50. *a* Converges Absolutely

51. *a* Radius=7, Interval $= (-10,4)$

52. *a* Radius $= \frac{1}{5}$, Interval $= \left[\frac{1}{5}, \frac{3}{5}\right]$

53. *a* Radius $= 2$, Interval $= (-5, -1)$

54. *a* Radius $= 7$, Interval $= (-12, 2]$

55. *a* Radius =1, Interval = $(-1,1)$

56. *a* Diverges by Integral test

57. *a* Diverges by Ratio test

58. *a* Converges by Limit Comparison

59. *a* Diverges by Limit Comparison/Integral Test

60. *a* Converges Absolutely by Alternating Series Test

61. *a* Diverges by Limit Comparison

62. *a* Converges by Direct Comparison/Integral Test

63. *a* Diverges by Ratio Test/Limit Comparison

64. *a* Diverges due to p-series

65. *a* Diverges by Integral Test

66. *a* Diverges by Ratio Test

67. *a* Converges by Integral Test/Ratio test

68. *a* Diverges by Ratio Test

69. *a* Converges by Ratio Test

70. *a* Diverges by Direct Comparison Test

71. *a* Converges by Ratio Test

72. *a* Diverges by Ratio Test

73. *a* Converges by Limit Comparison

74. *a* Converges by Ratio Test

75. a Converges Absolutely by Alternating Series Test

Chapter 10: Differential Equations

Separable Differential Equations, Logistic Models, Testing Solutions for Differential Equations, and Slope Fields

Separable Differential Equations

A differential equation is the derivative of a function. In order to solve a differential equation, the original function must be solved for. A separable differential equation is presented in the form below.

$$f(x)dx = g(y)dy$$

This can be solved by integrating both sides.

$$\int f(x)\, dx = \int g(y)\, dy$$

This simplifies to the form below.

$$F(x) = G(y) + C$$

If an initial value is given, substitute it into the final equation in order to solve for the constant of integration. The process of separating the variables and then integrating is further explained in the examples below.

10.1 $\dfrac{dy}{dx} = 3x$

Separate the x terms on one side, and the y terms on the other side as follows.

$$dy = 3xdx$$

Integrating both sides, we arrive at the function below.

$$\int dy = \int 3x\, dx$$

$$y = \frac{3}{2}x^2 + C$$

10.2 $\dfrac{dy}{dx} = \dfrac{y}{3x^2}$

Separate the variables of x onto one side of the equation, and the variables of y onto the other side.

$$\frac{1}{y}dy = \frac{1}{3x^2}dx$$

Integrating both sides, we arrive at the function below.

$$\int \frac{1}{y}dy = \int \frac{1}{3x^2}dx$$

$$\ln(y) = -\frac{1}{3x} + C$$

Solve for y by exponentiating both sides.

$$y = e^{-3x^{-1}+C}$$

This can be re-written in the form below.

$$y = Ce^{-3x^{-1}}$$

10.3 $\dfrac{dy}{dx} = \dfrac{\ln(x)}{y}$

Begin by separating the y and x terms.

$$y\,dy = \ln(x)\,dx$$

Integrating both sides gives the equations below.

$$\frac{1}{2}y^2 = x\ln(x) - x + C$$

$$y^2 = 2x\ln(x) - 2x + C$$

Since this is not a function, we can leave it how it is for the time being.

10. 4 $\dfrac{dy}{dx} = \dfrac{y}{1+x^2}$, and $y(0) = 1$

Being by separating the variables.

$$\frac{1}{y}dy = \frac{1}{1+x^2}dx$$

Integrating both sides gives the equation below.

$$\ln(y) = \arctan(x) + C$$

Exponentiating both sides gives the equation below.

$$y = Ce^{\arctan(x)}$$

Using the initial condition given allows us to solve for the constant of integration.

$$1 = C \cdot e^{\arctan(0)}$$

$$C = 1$$

Substitute this value back into the function.

$$y = e^{\arctan(x)}$$

The process of solving for the constant of integration using an initial condition is very simple, but should only be done after the differential equation is solved.

Logistic Curves

The logistic function is a type of differential equation that can be used to describe the growth of a variable, such as population or disease. The differential equation for the logistic function is given in the form below.

$$\frac{dy}{dt} = ky\left(1 - \frac{y}{L}\right)$$

Where k is a constant, and L is the carrying capacity.

Solving the separable differential equation above gives the function for logistic growth below.

$$y = \frac{L}{1 + Ce^{-kt}}$$

Graphing the slope field for the differential equation above along with the logistic growth function, we can see that as $t \to \infty, y \to L$. Additionally, the function is growing at the fastest rate when $y = \frac{L}{2}$.

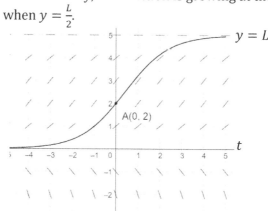

The slope field shown above is of $\frac{dy}{dx} = y\left(1 - \frac{y}{5}\right)$. From this differential equation, we can deduce that $k = 1$ and $L = 5$. Using this knowledge, the function graphed is of the form shown on the following page.

$$y = \frac{5}{1 + Ce^{-t}}.$$

In order to solve for C, we must use the initial condition of $(0, 2)$ given in the graph.

$$2 = \frac{5}{1 + Ce^0}$$

$$C = \frac{3}{2}$$

Therefore, the logistic growth model is equal to the function below.

$$y = \frac{5}{1 + \frac{3}{2}e^{-t}}$$

10.5 The population of cows in a certain farm is modeled by the logistic differential equation

$$\frac{dp}{dt} = kp\left(1 - \frac{p}{300}\right)$$

Where t is the number of years and p is the population of cows on the farm. Initially, 30 cows are kept on the farm. After 10 years, the number of cows on the farm grows to 150. The farm cannot hold more than 300 cows due to food and land constraints.

a) Determine the model for the number of cows on the farm in respect to years, t.

Since $L = 300$, the logistic model for the number of cows is of the form below.

$$y = \frac{300}{1 + Ce^{-kt}}$$

In order to solve for C, we can plug in the initial condition $y(0) = 30$.

$$30 = \frac{300}{1 + Ce^0}$$

$$C = 9$$

Therefore the model for the cow population is of the form below.

$$y = \frac{300}{1 + 9e^{-kt}}$$

To find the value of k in the model, we must use the second initial condition of $y(10) = 150$.

$$150 = \frac{300}{1 + 9e^{-10k}}$$

Solving for k gives $k \approx 0.220$. The equation can be rewritten in the form below.

$$y = \frac{300}{1 + 9e^{-0.220t}}$$

b) Draw a slope field for the logistic differential equation, and then graph the logistic function.

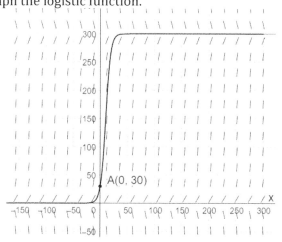

When the logistic function above is graphed, it intersects the y-axis at the point $(0,30)$, confirming that the function is a correct model for the number of cows on the farm.

c) Estimate the number of cows on the farm after 20 years.

The output value for $t = 20$ is of the form below.

$$y = \frac{300}{1 + 9e^{-0.220 \cdot 20}} = 270.150 \approx 270 \text{ cows}$$

d) Determine the limit as $t \to \infty$ for the logistic growth model.

$$\lim_{t \to \infty} \frac{300}{1 + 9e^{-0.220t}} = \frac{300}{1} = 300$$

e) Determine the point on the logistic growth model where the population of cows is growing at the fastest rate.

The population grows at the fastest when $y = \frac{L}{2}$. In this case, the population of cows grows fastest at $y = 150$. The corresponding value of t is 9.987 years.

Testing Solutions for Differential Equations

When a solution is given to a differential equation, we can take its derivatives and substitute them into the differential equation.

10.8 $y'' + y' = 0$, confirm that $y = e^{-x}$ is a solution to the differential equation.

Start by taking the first and second derivatives of e^{-x}.

$$y = e^{-x}$$
$$y' = -e^{-x}$$
$$y'' = e^{-x}$$

Substituting these values into the original differential equation, we arrive at the equation below.

$$e^{-x} + (-e^{-x}) = 0$$

$$0 = 0$$

This confirms that the solution given is correct.

10.9 $x^2 y'' + xy' = 0$, confirm that $y = \ln(x)$ is a solution to the differential equation.

The derivatives of the solution are as follows.

$$y = \ln(x)$$

$$y' = \frac{1}{x}$$

$$y'' = -\frac{1}{x^2}$$

Substituting these values back into the differential equation gives the following.

$$x^2 \cdot -\frac{1}{x^2} + x \cdot \frac{1}{x} = 0$$

$$-1 + 1 = 0$$

$$0 = 0$$

This confirms that the given solution is correct.

10. 10 $y''' + 4y'' + 2y' + 8y = 0$, confirm if $y = e^{-4x}$ and $y = e^{4x}$ are both solutions of the differential equation.

The first, second, and third derivatives of e^{-4x} and e^{4x} are shown below.

$$y = e^{-4x}, y' = -4e^{-4x}, y'' = 16e^{-4x}, y''' = -64e^{-4x}$$

$$y = e^{4x}, y' = 4e^{4x}, y'' = 16e^{4x}, y''' = 64e^{4x}$$

Substituting the first solution into the differential equation, we arrive at the form below.

$$(-64e^{-4x}) + 4(16e^{-4x}) + 2(-4e^{-4x}) + 8(e^{-4x}) = 0$$

$$-64e^{-4x} + 64e^{-4x} - 8e^{-4x} + 8e^{-4x} = 0$$

$$0 = 0$$

This confirms that $y = e^{-4x}$ is a valid solution for the differential equation. Now, testing $y = e^{4x}$, we arrive at the form below.

$$(64e^{4x}) + 4(16e^{4x}) + 2(4e^{4x}) + 8(e^{4x}) = 0$$

$$64e^{4x} + 64e^{4x} + 8e^{4x} + 8e^{4x} = 0$$

$$144e^{4x} = 0$$

Since the equation is not true, $y = e^{4x}$ is not a valid solution to the differential equation.

Slope Fields

A slope field, also known as a direction field, maps the general solution to a differential equation in the form below.

$$\frac{dy}{dx} = f(x, y)$$

The slope field of the function $y = x^2$ is shown below.

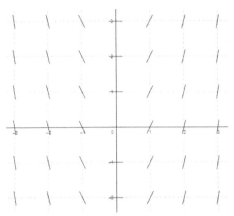

The derivative of this function is as follows.

$$\frac{dy}{dx} = 2x$$

At each point on the graph, the slope of the line segment drawn is equal to two times the value of the x-coordinate.

Some possible solution curves for the slope field above are shown in the graph on the following page. The series of curves are called isoclines. The isoclines represent possible solutions to the differential equation $\frac{dy}{dx} = 2x$. The differing solutions shown in the graph below are present due to the constant of integration that arises from solving the given differential equation.

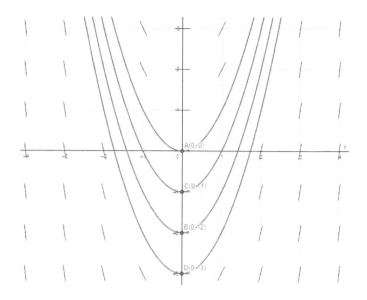

10. 11 Sketch the slope field for $\dfrac{dy}{dx} = 3x^2$.

We can check the function represented by the slope field by solving the differential equation. In this case, the function is $y = x^3 + C$. The slope field is drawn by making line segments with a slope of $3x^2$ at the given x-coordinate. This process is shown below.

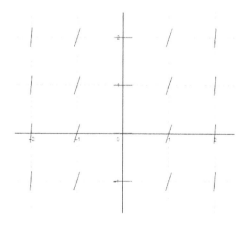

A possible solution curve to this slope field is shown below.

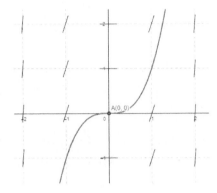

You can find practice problems for this chapter beginning on the next page.

Chapter 10 Practice Problems

Solve each of the following differential equations. Identify the value of the constant of integration if an initial condition is given in the problem.

1. $\dfrac{dy}{dx} = 7x$

2. $\dfrac{dy}{dx} = \dfrac{2x}{4 + x^2}$

3. $\dfrac{dy}{dx} \cdot \dfrac{1}{x} = 7x^2 + 5$

4. $\dfrac{dy}{dx} = \dfrac{3y}{7x}$

5. $\dfrac{dy}{dx} = -\dfrac{x}{y}$

6. $\dfrac{dy}{dx} \cdot \dfrac{1}{y} = \ln(x)$

7. $\dfrac{dy}{dx} \cdot \dfrac{2y^3}{y^4} = \arctan(x)$

8. $\dfrac{dy}{dx} = x \cdot \ln(x) + 5$

9. $\dfrac{dy}{dx} = \dfrac{y^2}{3x}$

10. $\dfrac{dy}{dx} \cdot \arctan(y) = \dfrac{1}{1 + x^2}$

11. $\dfrac{dy}{dx} = \sin^5(x)\cos(x), \quad y\left(\dfrac{3\pi}{2}\right) = \dfrac{19}{6}$

12. $\dfrac{dy}{dx} = 7y\tan(x), \quad y(0) = 128$

13. $\dfrac{dy}{dx} = 2y \cdot xe^x, \quad y(0) = e^2$

14. $\dfrac{dy}{dx} = y^2 \cdot \ln(x) \cdot x^{-1}, \quad y(e) = \dfrac{1}{3}$

15. $\dfrac{dy}{dx} = \dfrac{y}{x^2 + 5x + 6}, \quad y(0) = 2$

Use the following scenario to answer questions 16-20.

The number of bacteria at the beginning of an experiment is equal to 8. The number of bacteria after 2 hours of experimentation is equal to 64. The logistic differential equation for this scenario is given as

$$\frac{dB}{dt} = kB\left(1 - \frac{B}{1000}\right)$$

Where B is the number of bacteria in the experiment, and t is the amount of time in hours.

16. Determine the carrying capacity of bacteria for this experiment.

17. Give a model for the growth of bacteria in terms of t.

18. Graph the equation for the number of bacteria in the experiment versus the time in hours, and draw the appropriate asymptote.

19. Use the model to determine the number of bacteria in the the experiment after 5 hours.

20. Find the limit of the number of bacteria in the experiment at $t \to \infty$.

Use the following scenario to answer questions 21-25.

The number of students in a school who have heard a secret at the beginning of the day is 4. After 1 hour, the number of people who have heard the same secret is equal to 25. The logistic differential equation for this scenario is given as follows.

$$\frac{dS}{dt} = kS\left(1 - \frac{S}{1200}\right)$$

Where S is the number of students who have heard the secret, and t is the time in hours.

21. Write a model for the number of students who know the secret in terms of t.

22. If the original number of students who heard the secret after 1 hour is equal to 8, what is the new value of k?

23. What is the carrying capacity, or maximum number of students who can hear the secret according to the original model?

24. Sketch the graph of the number of students who have heard the secret against the time t in hours using the model from question 21.

25. At what time is the rate of the spread of the rumor at a maximum using the model from question 21?

Use the following scenario to answer questions 26-30.

The number of fish placed in a newly created pond is equal to 200. After 50 days, the number of fish in this pond is equal to 500. The differential equation given for this scenario is of the form below.

$$\frac{dF}{dt} = kF\left(1 - \frac{F}{10000}\right)$$

Where F is the number of fish in the pond, and t is the time elapsed in days.

26. Determine the carrying capacity of the pond.

27. Give a model for the number of fish in the pond in terms of the time elapsed in days.

28. Use this model to determine the number of fish in the pond after 500 days.

29. If the initial number of fish placed into this pond was 12,000, how many fish would remain as $t \to \infty$.

30. Determine the point at which the number of fish had the highest rate of change from the model in question 27.

31. $y'' - y' - 30y = 0$, verify that $y = e^{-5x}$ is a solution to the differential equation.

32. $y''' + 12y'' + 47y' + 60y = 0$, verify that $y = e^{-3x}$, $y = e^{-4x}$, and $y = e^{-6x}$ are all solutions to the differential equation.

33. $y'' - 4y' + 4y = 0$, verify that $y = xe^{2x}$ is a solution to the differential equation.

34. $y^{(4)} + 8y''' + 24y'' + 32y' + 16y = 0$, verify that $y = x^3 e^{-2x}$ is a solution to the differential equation.

35. $y^{(4)} - y = 0$, verify that $y = \cos(x)$ is a solution to the differential equation.

36. Sketch the slope field for $\dfrac{dy}{dx} = 3x^2$ on the graph below.

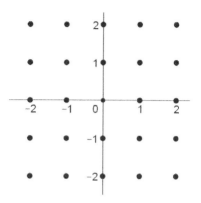

37. Sketch the slope field for $\dfrac{dy}{dx} = 6x + e^x$ on the graph below.

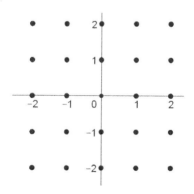

38. Sketch the slope field for $\dfrac{dy}{dx} = \sin(x)$ on the graph below.

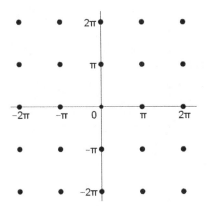

39. Sketch the slope field for $\dfrac{dy}{dx} = \cos(x)$ on the graph below.

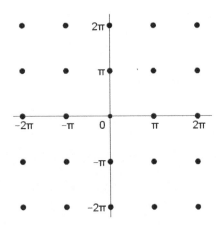

40. Skech the slope field for $\dfrac{dy}{dx} = \dfrac{1}{x}$ on the graph below.

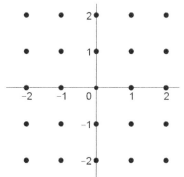

41. The slope field below is for the differential equation $\dfrac{dy}{dx} = -\dfrac{x}{y}$. Sketch a possible solution to this equation.

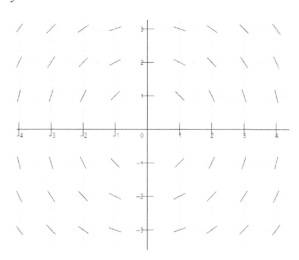

42. The slope field below is for the differential equation $\dfrac{dy}{dx} = \dfrac{1}{x}$. Sketch a possible solution to this equation.

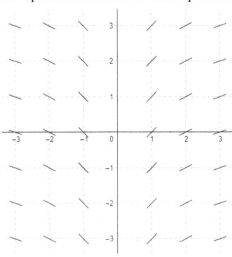

43. The slope field below is for the differential equation $\dfrac{dy}{dx} = \dfrac{1}{1+x^2}$. Sketch a possible solution to this equation.

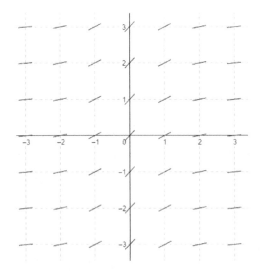

44. The slope field below is for the differential equation $\frac{dy}{dx} = x^2 e^x$. Sketch a possible solution to this equation.

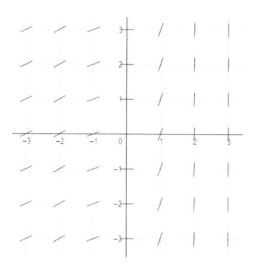

45. The slope field below is for the differential equation $\frac{dy}{dx} = \sec^2(x)$. Sketch a possible solution to this equation.

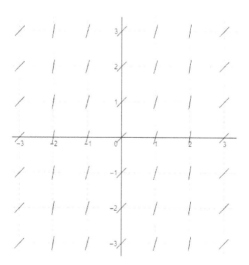

46 – 50. Match the slope field with the corresponding equation.

46. $y = x^2$

47. $y = \dfrac{1}{x^3}$

48. $y = -\cos(x)$

49. $y = \dfrac{1}{1 + x^2}$

50. $y = e^{2x}$

 I.

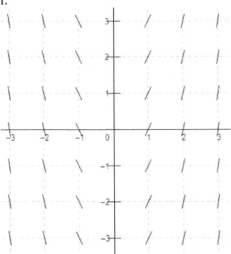

II.

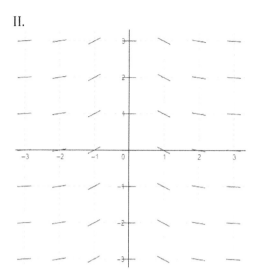

III.

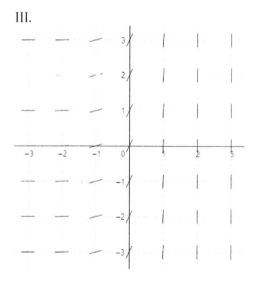

IV.

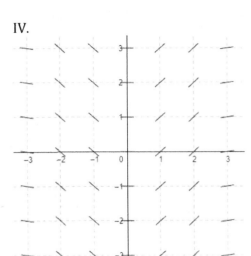

V.

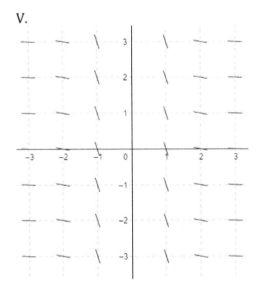

Chapter 10 Practice Problem Answers

1. a $y = \frac{7}{2}x^2 + C$

2. a $y = \ln|x^2 + 4| + C$

3. a $y = \frac{7}{4}x^4 + \frac{5}{2}x^2 + C$

4. a $y^{\frac{1}{3}} = Cx^{\frac{1}{7}}$

5. a $x^2 + y^2 = C$

6. a $y = Ce^{(x\ln(x)-x)}$

7. a $y = Ce^{\frac{1}{2}x\arctan(x)-\frac{1}{4}\ln|x^2+1|}$

8. a $y = \frac{1}{2}x^2\ln(x) - \frac{1}{4}x^2 + 5x + C$

9. a $y = -\frac{3}{\ln(x)+C}$

10. a $y\arctan(y) - \frac{1}{2}\ln|1 + y^2| = \arctan(x) + C$

11. a $y = \frac{1}{6}\sin^6(x) + 3$

12. a $y = \frac{128}{\cos^7(x)}$

13. a $y = e^{(2xe^x-2e^x+4)}$

14. a $y = -\frac{2}{\ln^2(x)-7}$

15. a $y = \frac{3|x+2|}{|x+3|}$

16. a 1000

17. a $y = \dfrac{1000}{1+124e^{-1.068t}}$

18. a

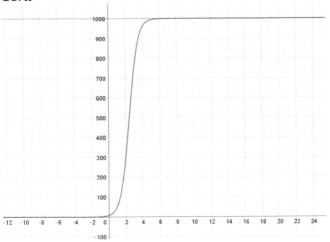

19. a 627 bacteria (Rounded to nearest whole number)

20. a 1000

21. a $S = \dfrac{1200}{1+299e^{-1.850t}}$

22. a $k = 0.696$

23. a 1200

24. a

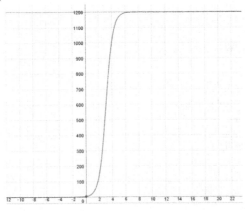

25. a $t = 3.081, S = 600$

26. a 10,000

27. a $F = \dfrac{10000}{1+49e^{-0.019t}}$

28. a 9963 fish(Rounded to nearest whole number)

29. a 10,000

30. a $t = 204.83, F = 5000$

31. a e^{-5x} is a valid solution

32. a e^{-3x} and e^{-4x} are valid solutions. e^{-6x} is not a valid solution

33. a xe^{2x} is a valid solution

34. a $x^3 e^{-2x}$ is a valid solution

35. a $\cos(x)$ is a valid solution

36. a

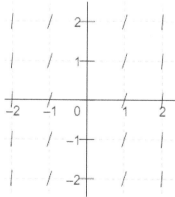

37. *a*

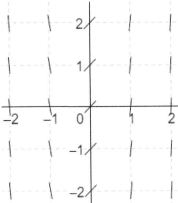

38. *a*

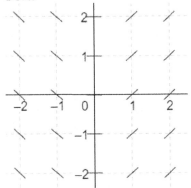

39. *a*

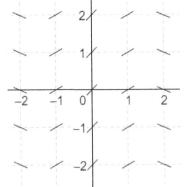

40. a

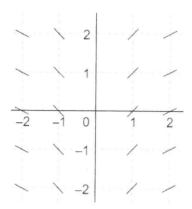

41. a

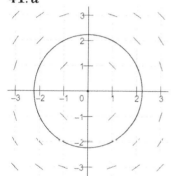

42. a

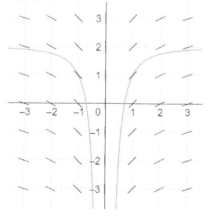

43. a

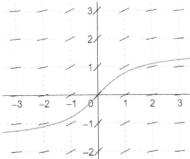

44. a

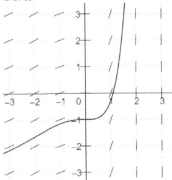

45. a

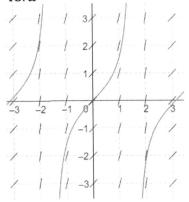

46. *a* I

47. *a* V

48. *a* IV

49. *a* II

50. *a* III

AP BC Calculus Practice Test

Test Format			
Section I Part A	30 Questions	60 Minutes	No Calculator
Section I Part B	15 Questions	45 Minutes	Calculator Required
Section II Part A	2 Questions	30 Minutes	Calculator Required
Section II Part B	4 Questions	60 Minutes	No Calculator

Section I and Section II are each weighted 50% of the total exam score.

A CALCULATOR MAY NOT BE USED ON THIS PART OF THE
EXAM.

Directions: Solve each of the following problems and select the
correct answer. There is only one correct answer choice for
each problem.

Notes:

(1) Unless specified, the domain of a given function f is
assumed to be the set of all real numbers x for which $f(x)$ is a
real number.

(2) The inverse of a function f is denoted as f^{-1} or by the
prefix "arc." (ex. $\arcsin(x) = \sin^{-1}(x)$)

1. Evaluate the derivative for the following function.

$$f(x) = \ln(2x) + 6$$

A) $f'(x) = \dfrac{1}{2x}$

B) $f'(x) = \dfrac{1}{x} + 6x$

C) $f'(x) = \dfrac{1}{x}$

D) $f'(x) = \ln(2x)$

2. Identify the equation of the line tangent to the point at $x = 0$ for the function below.

$$f(x) = 4\arctan(2x)$$

A) $y - \dfrac{\pi}{4} = 8x$

B) $y = 8x$

C) $y - \dfrac{\pi}{2} = 4x$

D) $y = 4x$

3. $\displaystyle\int [\tan(x) + \sec^2(x)]dx =$

A) $- \ln|\cos(x)| - \tan(x) + C$

B) $\ln|\sec(x)| - \tan(x) + C$

C) $\ln|\sec(x)| + \tan(x) + C$

D) $\ln|\cos(x)| + \tan(x) + C$

4. $\displaystyle\int_{0}^{1} \frac{4}{1+x^2}\,dx =$

A) 0

B) 1

C) $\dfrac{\pi}{2}$

D) π

5. Identify the time where the position function below reaches its minimum velocity, $t \geq 0$.

$$s(t) = t^4 - 3t^3 - 6t^2 + 27t$$

A) $t = 2$

B) $t = \dfrac{9}{4}$

C) $t = 3$

D) $t = -\dfrac{1}{2}$

6. A plane flying at 105 feet off the ground travels away from a 5-foot-tall boy on the ground at a rate of 500 feet per second. If the boy watches the plane fly away from him after passing directly over him, at what rate is the angle of his eyes changing when the plane is 100 feet away from him?

A) $\dfrac{1}{26}$ radians per second

B) $\dfrac{5}{2}$ radians per second

C) $\dfrac{1}{200}$ radians per second

D) $\dfrac{50000}{(20,000)^{\frac{1}{2}}}$ feet per second

7. $\dfrac{d}{dx}\left[\displaystyle\int_{0}^{x^2+7x} \sin(t)\cos(t)\,dt\right] =$

A) $\sin(x^2 + 7x) \cdot \cos(x^2 + 7x)$

B) $\dfrac{1}{2}\sin(x^2 + 7x)$

C) $\dfrac{1}{2}\sin(2x^2 + 14x) \cdot (2x + 7)$

D) $\dfrac{1}{2}\sin(2x^2 + 14x) \cdot \left(\dfrac{1}{3}x^3 + \dfrac{7}{2}x^2\right)$

8. $\displaystyle\lim_{x \to \infty} \dfrac{x^3}{\ln(x)} =$

A) $-\infty$

B) $3x^3$

C) 3

D) DNE

9. $\int \dfrac{2 + 2x}{1 - x^2}\,dx =$

A) $-2\ln|2 + x| + C$

B) $2\ln|1 - x| + C$

C) $-2\ln|1 - x| + C$

D) $2\ln|2 + x| + C$

10. Use the following table to calculate the trapezoidal sum of the area under the curve on the interval $[0,4]$, $(\Delta x = 1)$.

x	0	1	2	3	4
$f(x)$	7	7	3	4	2

A) $\dfrac{37}{4}$

B) 16

C) $\dfrac{37}{2}$

D) 21

11. Which of the following answer choices is a solution to the differential equation below?

$$y''' - 6y'' + 11y' - 6y = 0$$

A) $y = e^{-x}$

B) $y = e^{4x}$

C) $y = e^{-3x}$

D) $y = e^{3x}$

12. Determine the average value under the function $f(x) = 3x \cos(x)$ on the interval $[0, \pi]$.

A) $-\dfrac{6}{\pi}$

B) $\dfrac{6}{\pi}$

C) $\dfrac{3}{\pi}$

D) $\dfrac{-3}{\pi}$

13. $\int \sin^7(x)\cot(x)dx =$

A) $\frac{1}{7}\cos^7(x) + C$

B) $\frac{1}{7}\sin^7(x) + C$

C) $\frac{1}{8}\sin^8(x) + C$

D) $\frac{1}{8}\cos^8(x) + C$

14. $\int_{2}^{3} x^2\sqrt{x^3 - 7}\, dx =$

A) $\frac{2}{9}(20)^{\frac{3}{2}} - \frac{2}{9}$

B) $\frac{2}{9}(1)^{\frac{3}{2}} - \frac{2}{9}$

C) $\frac{2}{9}(37)^{\frac{3}{2}} - \frac{2}{9}$

D) $\frac{2}{9}(2)^{\frac{3}{2}} - \frac{2}{9}$

15. Identify extrema for the following function.

$$f(x) = 3x^3 + \frac{45}{2}x^2 + 54x + 3$$

A) Relative Maximum at $x = -3$,
Relative Minimum at $x = -2$

B) Relative Minimum at $x = -3$,
Relative Maximum at $x = -2$

C) Absolute Maximum at $x = -3$,
Absolute Minimum at $x = -2$

D) Absolute Minimum at $x = -3$,
Absolute Maximum at $x = -2$

16. Which value of c below satisfies the Mean Value Theorem for the function below on $[3,5]$?

$$f(x) = x^2 - 6x + 15$$

A) 4

B) 3

C) 0

D) $\frac{10}{3}$

17. $\int \dfrac{2x}{\sqrt{16 - x^4}}\,dx =$

A) $\arctan\left(\dfrac{x^2}{4}\right) + C$

B) $\text{arcsec}\left(\dfrac{x^2}{2}\right) + C$

C) $\arccos\left(\dfrac{x^2}{4}\right) + C$

D) $\arcsin\left(\dfrac{x^2}{4}\right) + C$

18. Solve the following differential equation given the initial value.

$$\frac{dy}{dx} = \tan(x), y(0) = 1$$

A) $y = \ln|\cos(x)| + 1$

B) $y = \ln|\cos(x)|$

C) $y = -\ln|\cos(x)| + 1$

D) $y = -\ln|\cos(x)| - 1$

19. $\int x^4 \cos(x)\, dx =$

A) $-x^4 \cos(x) + 4x^3 \cos(x) + 12x^2 \cos(x) + 24x\cos(x)$
$\quad\quad - 24\sin(x)$

B) $x^4 \sin(x) + 4x^3 \cos(x) - 12x^2 \sin(x) - 24x\cos(x)$
$\quad\quad + 24\sin(x)$

C) $-x^4 \sin(x) - 4x^3 \cos(x) + 12x^2 \sin(x) + 24x\cos(x) -$
$24\sin(x)$

D) $-x^4 \sin(x) - 4x^3 \cos(x) + 12x^2 \sin(x) + 24x\cos(x)$
$\quad\quad + 24\cos(x)$

20. Find the length of the arc for t values $[1,4]$ for the parametric equations below.

$$y = 4\cos(2t)$$
$$x = 4\sin(2t)$$

A) 32

B) 40

C) 24

D) 12

21. Determine the appropriate Maclaurin Series for $f(x) = \sin(2x)$ from the choices below.

A) $2x - \dfrac{4}{3}x^3 + \dfrac{4}{15}x^5 - \dfrac{8}{315}x^7 \ldots$

B) $x^2 - \dfrac{2}{3}x^6 + \dfrac{2}{15}x^8 - \dfrac{4}{315}x^{10}$

C) $\dfrac{x}{2} - \dfrac{1}{24}x^3 + \dfrac{1}{240}x^5 - \dfrac{1}{10080}x^7$

D) $1 - 2x^2 + \dfrac{2}{3}x^4 - \dfrac{4}{45}x^6 + \dfrac{2}{315}x^8 \ldots$

22. Which of the following integrals properly identifies the volume of the solid formed by the revolution of the area between the curves $y = x^3$ and $y = x$ around the x-axis?

A) $\pi \displaystyle\int_0^1 ((x^3)^2 - (x)^2)dx$

B) $\pi \displaystyle\int_0^1 (x^3 - x^2)dx$

C) $\pi \displaystyle\int_0^1 ((x)^2 - (x^3)^2)dx$

D) $2\pi \displaystyle\int_0^1 ((x^3)^2 - (x)^2)dx$

23. $xy = 2x^2 + 3y$.

Solve for $\frac{dy}{dx}$

A) $\dfrac{4x - y + 3}{x}$

B) $\dfrac{y - 3x}{3}$

C) $\dfrac{4x - y}{x - 3}$

D) $\dfrac{x - y}{4x - 3}$

24. If a vector function is defined by the function below, then find $f''(t)$.

$$f(t) = \langle -\sin(3t), \cos^2(3t) \rangle$$

A) $\langle 9\sin(3t), -18\cos(6t) \rangle$

B) $\langle 3\cos(3t), -3\sin(6t) \rangle$

C) $\langle 9\cos(3t), -18\sin(6t) \rangle$

D) $\langle -18\cos(3t), 9\sin(6t) \rangle$

25.

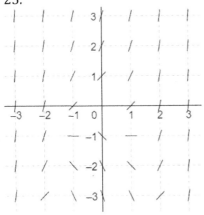

The slope field above is of which of the following differential equations?

A) $\dfrac{dy}{dx} = x + y$

B) $\dfrac{dy}{dx} = x^2 + y$

C) $\dfrac{dy}{dx} = x + y^2$

D) $\dfrac{dy}{dx} = x^2 + y^2$

26. What is the area under the curve for the following parametric equation?

$$r = 2 + 2\cos(\theta)$$

A) 6π

B) 2π

B) 12π

D) 4π

27. $\displaystyle\int_{1}^{\infty} \frac{1}{x^2 + 4}\,dx =$

A) $\dfrac{3\pi}{8}$

B) $\dfrac{-3\pi}{8}$

C) $\dfrac{\pi}{4} - \dfrac{1}{2}\arctan\left(\dfrac{1}{2}\right)$

D) $\dfrac{\pi}{2} - \dfrac{1}{2}\arctan\left(\dfrac{1}{2}\right)$

28. Find the maximum r value for the polar curve below.

$r = 2 + 4\sin(\theta)$

A) 2

B) 6

C) 4

D) 8

29. $\displaystyle\sum_{n=0}^{\infty} 4\left(\frac{1}{3}\right)^{n+1} =$

A) $\dfrac{2}{3}$

B) 2

C) 6

D) 12

30. Which of the following values for x will cause the following series to converge?

$$\sum_{n=0}^{\infty} \frac{2^n (x + 2)^n}{(n + 1)}$$

A) $-\dfrac{5}{2}$

B) $-\dfrac{3}{2}$

C) $\dfrac{3}{2}$

D) $\dfrac{5}{2}$

CALCULUS BC
SECTION I, Part B
Time - 45 minutes
Number of questions – 15

A CALCULATOR IS REQUIRED FOR SOME QUESTIONS ON THIS PART OF THE EXAM.

Directions: Solve each of the following problems and select the correct answer. There is only one correct answer choice for each problem.

1. Calculate the volume formed by the revolution of the function below around the y-axis. The function is bounded by the x-axis, y-axis, and $x = 3.5$.

$$f(x) = \frac{3}{(x+1)^2} + e^x$$

A) 540.150

B) 216.448

C) 1791.035

D) 3582.070

2. Identify the acceleration of the particle given by the position function below at time $t = 7.6$.

$$s(t) = \ln(t^2) + \ln(\sin(t))$$

A) $- 15.875$

B) $- 0.303$

C) $- 1.102$

D) 0.523

3. Solve for y given $\dfrac{dy}{dx} = \tan^2(x), y(0) = 1$

A) $y = \tan(x) - x + 1$

B) $y = \tan(x) - x - 1$

C) $y = \sec^2(x) + x + 1$

D) $y = \sec^2(x) - x + 1$

4. Find the bounded area between the two functions below.

$$f(x) = \sqrt{x}$$

$$f(x) = x^2$$

A) $\frac{1}{3}$

B) $-\frac{1}{3}$

C) $\frac{2}{3}$

D) $-\frac{2}{3}$

5. Approximate the value of $f(1.5)$ using Euler's Method, where $n = 5$ and $f(1) = 2$.

$$f'(x) = x\ln(x) - x$$

A) 1.606

B) 1.514

C) 1.424

D) 1.519

6. At what time(s) does the velocity of the particle given by the parametric equations below equal 0 within the first 25 seconds?

$$y = 20\sin(\sqrt{t})$$

$$x = 3t$$

A) $t = 2.467$

B) $t = 22.207$

C) $t = 2.467, t = 22.207$

D) $t = 9.870$

7. The average value of $f(x) = e^x$ on the interval $[1,5]$ is equal to which of the following?

A) 12.970

B) 36.423

C) 36.424

D) 36.853

8. $\int \dfrac{2}{(x^3 + 5x^2 + 6x)}\,dx$

A) $\dfrac{1}{3}\ln|x| - \ln|x + 2| + \dfrac{2}{3}\ln|x + 3| + C$

B) $\dfrac{1}{3}\ln|x + 3| - \ln|x + 2| + \dfrac{2}{3}\ln|x| + C$

C) $\dfrac{1}{3}\ln|x + 2| - \ln|x| + \dfrac{2}{3}\ln|x + 3| + C$

D) $\dfrac{2}{3}\ln|x| - \ln|x + 2| + \dfrac{1}{3}\ln|x + 3| + C$

9. $\lim\limits_{n \to \infty} \dfrac{n^2}{2^n}$

A) 0

B) 2

C) ∞

D) n

10. Using Euler's Method, approximate the function value for $f(x) = x^3 + 7x^2 + 3x$ at $x = 2$, using a step value of 0.2, and starting with the value at $x = 1$.

A) 31.00

B) 39.72

C) 40.86

D) 48.32

11. Determine the interval of convergence for the following series

$$\sum_{n-0}^{\infty} \frac{(n-1)(x+2)^{n+1}}{(n+5)}.$$

A) $[-3, -1]$

B) $(-3, -1]$

C) $[-3, -1)$

D) $(-3, -1)$

12. A soldier drops a bomb out of an airplane at 537 feet of altitude travelling parallel to the ground. The bomb falls at a rate of 32 feet per second due to gravity, while the plane travels away from the bomb at a rate of 731 feet per second. At what rate is the distance between the plane and the bomb changing when the bomb hits the ground?

A) 731.700 feet per second

B) 728.901 feet per second

C) 1.043 feet per second

D) 12278.842 feet per second

13. Find the position of the particle at time $t = 3$ for the particle given by the velocity function below. The particle is at 0 when $t = 1$.

$$v(t) = \sin((\ln(t))^2)$$

A) 1.914

B) 1.184

C) 2.184

D) 0.914

14. Find the area between the two polar curves below.

$$r = 4$$

$$r = 3 + 2\sin(\theta)$$

A) 11.515

B) 28.535

C) 34.558

D) 15.708

15. Find the slope of the line tangent to the parametric curve at $t = 6$.

$$x = 4\sin(t^2)$$

$$y = e^t + t^2$$

A) $-$ 67.635

B) 10.698

C) $-$ 1.954

D) $-$ 8.727

A graphing calculator is required for these problems.

1. The number of amoeba in a scientific experiment is modeled by the differential equation below.

$$\frac{dA}{dt} = kA\left(1 - \frac{A}{400}\right)$$

Where t is the number of hours, and A is the number of amoeba in the experiment. Initially, there are 120 amoeba in the experiment. After 5 hours of experimentation, there are 300 amoeba.

(a) Determine the model for the number of amoeba in the experiment with respect to time in hours.

(b) Estimate the number of amoeba after 7 hours of experimentation.

(c) Determine the limit as $t \to \infty$ for the growth model of amoeba.

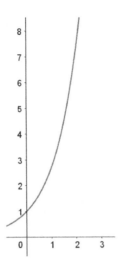

2. Above is the curve for $y = e^x$ restricted by the y-axis and $y = e^3$.

(a) Find the volume formed by revolving the curve around the y-axis.

(b) The revolved shape forms the shape of a canister used to store water. The volume calculated in part (a) is a measurement in gallons. Water flows into the canister at 2 gallons per minute. What is the rate of change of the radius of the water in the canister when there are 217 gallons in the canister? Hint: $\int xe^x = xe^x - e^x + C$

CALCULUS BC
SECTION II, Part B
Time - 60 minutes
Number of questions – 4

A graphing calculator is not allowed for these problems.

3. Consider the differential equation $\frac{dy}{dx} = x^3 - 2y^2$.

(a) Sketch the slope field for the differential equation on the graph provided below.

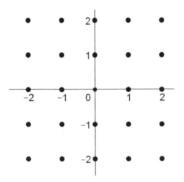

(b) Find $\frac{d^2y}{dx^2}$ in terms of x and y. Determine the concavity of the possible solution curves to the differential equation in the second quadrant based on your answer.

(c) Let $f = g(x)$ be a particular solution to the differential equation with $g(0) = 1$. Use Euler's method, starting at $x = 0$ with $n = 5$ to estimate the value of $g(5)$.

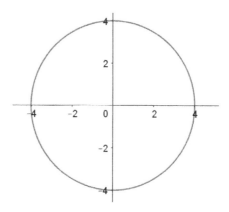

4. Above is the graph of the parametric curve $r = 4$.

(a) Convert the curve from parametric to Cartesian form.
(b) Find the location(s) on the polar curve where $x = 2$ from $0 \leq \theta \leq 2\pi$.
(c) This parametric curve is the derivative for the curve $r = 4\theta$. What do the values of $r = 4$ for $0 \leq \theta \leq 2\pi$ mean for the curve's antiderivative?
(d) Find the area under $r = 4\theta$ from $0 \leq \theta \leq 2\pi$.
(e) The curve $r = 4\theta$ represents a model for the growth of plants, where the length of r is the growth of the plant in centimeters at a specific day θ. Find the length of a plant growing according to this model 5 days after being planted.

5. A particle moves along the x-axis over time, t, in seconds by the equation below. $t \geq 0$

$$s(t) = t^3 - 6t^2 + 9t - 18$$

(a) Find the velocity and acceleration functions for the particle.
(b) When is the particle at rest?
(c) When is the particle moving in the forward direction?
(d) When is the particle increasing in speed?
(e) When is the particle moving the fastest in the backwards direction?
(f) Find the total distance travelled by the particle after 5 seconds.

6. Consider the following Maclaurin series for the function f.

$$\sum_{n=1}^{\infty} \frac{(-2)^{n+1}}{n+1} x^n = 2x - \frac{8}{3}x^2 + 4x^3 + \cdots \frac{(-2)^{n+1}}{n+1} x^n + \cdots$$

(a) Use the ratio test to determine the radius and interval of convergence for the series above.

(b) Write the first three nonzero terms of the Maclaurin series for F, the antiderivative of f.

(c) Write the first three nonzero terms of the Maclaurin series for $\cos(x)$. Use this series to write the third degree Maclaurin polynomial for $h(x) = \cos(x) f(x)$.

Multiple Choice Answer Key – Section I Part A

1. C
2. B
3. C
4. D
5. A
6. B
7. C
8. D
9. C
10. C
11. D
12. A
13. B
14. A
15. A
16. A
17. D
18. C
19. B
20. C
21. A
22. C
23. C
24. A
25. B
26. A
27. C
28. B
29. B
30. A

Multiple Choice Answer Key- Section I Part B

1. A
2. C
3. A
4. A
5. B
6. C
7. C
8. A
9. A
10. B
11. D
12. A
13. D
14. B
15. A

Section II Part A Scoring Guidelines
AP Calculus BC Scoring Guidelines Question 1
The number of amoeba in a scientific experiment is modeled by the differential equation below.

$$\frac{dA}{dt} = kA\left(1 - \frac{A}{400}\right)$$

Where t is the number of hours, and A is the number of amoeba in the experiment. Initially, there are 120 amoeba in the experiment. After 5 hours of experimentation, there are 300 amoeba.

  (a) Determine the model for the number of amoeba in the experiment with respect to time in hours.
  (b) Estimate the number of amoeba after 7 hours of experimentation.
  (c) Determine the limit as $t \to \infty$ for the growth model of amoeba.

(a) $y = \frac{400}{1+Ce^{-kt}}$ $y(0) = 120, y(5) = 300$ $C = \frac{7}{3}$ $k = 0.389$ $y = \frac{400}{1+\frac{7}{3}e^{-0.389t}}$	$5:\begin{cases} 1: \text{Correct logistic function} \\ 1: \text{Correct initial conditions} \\ 1: \text{Correct C value} \\ 1: \text{Correct } k \text{ value} \\ 1: \text{Correct final} \\ \quad \text{growth model} \end{cases}$
(b) $y = \frac{400}{1+\frac{7}{3}e^{-0.389\cdot7}} =$ 347(rounded to nearest whole number)	$2:\begin{cases} 1: \text{Correct Substitution} \\ 1: \text{Correct estimation} \end{cases}$
(c) The limit as the function approaches infinity is equal to carrying capacity, or L. In this growth model, $L = 400$.	$2:\begin{cases} 1: \text{Evaluate limit} \\ 1: \text{Justification} \end{cases}$

AP AB/BC Calculus Scoring Guidelines Question 2

Above is the curve for $y = e^x$ restricted by the y-axis and $y = e^3$.

(a) Find the volume formed by revolving the curve around the y-axis.

(b) The revolved shape forms the shape of a canister used to store water. The volume calculated in part (a) is a measurement in gallons. Water flows into the canister at 2 gallons per minute. What is the rate of change of the radius of the water in the canister when there are 217 gallons in the canister? Hint: $\int xe^x = xe^x - e^x + C$

(a) $V = 2\pi \int_0^3 x(e^3 - e^x)dx$

$V = 5\pi e^3 - 2\pi \approx 309.220$

$2:\begin{cases} 1: \text{Correct integral} \\ 1: \text{Answer (exact BC only)} \end{cases}$

(b) $V = 2\pi \int_0^{x_1} x(e^3 - e^x)dx$

$\dfrac{dV}{dt} = \dfrac{d\left(2\pi \int_0^{x_1} x(e^3 - e^x)dx\right)}{dt}$

$= 2\pi x_1(e^3 - e^{x_1}) \cdot \dfrac{dx}{dt} = 2$

$V = 217 = 2\pi \int_0^{x_1} x(e^3 - e^x)dx$

$= \pi x_1^2 e^3 - 2\pi x_1 e^{x_1} + 2\pi e^{x_1} - 2\pi$

$x_1 = 2.109$

Radius $= x_1 = 2.109$

$\dfrac{dx}{dt} = \dfrac{2}{2\pi x_1(e^3 - e^{x_1})}$

$= 0.013 \dfrac{\text{units}}{\text{minute}}$

$7:\begin{cases} 1: \text{Correct Volume} \\ \quad \text{Derivative} \\ 1: \text{2nd Fundamental} \\ \quad \text{Theorem} \\ 1: \text{Correct } x_1 \text{ value} \\ 1: \text{Correct Radius} \\ \quad \text{and } x_1 = \text{radius} \\ 1: \text{Improper Integral} \\ 1: \text{Correct Radius} \\ 1: \text{Answer} \\ (\text{units not required}) \end{cases}$

Section II Part B Scoring Guidelines
AP Calculus BC Scoring Guidelines Question 3

Consider the differential equation $\frac{dy}{dx} = x^3 - 2y^2$.

(a) Sketch the slope field for the differential equation on the graph provided below.

(b) Find $\frac{d^2y}{dx^2}$ in terms of x and y. Determine the concavity of the possible solution curves to the differential equation in the second quadrant based on your answer.

(c) Let $f = g(x)$ be a particular solution to the differential equation with $g(0) = 1$. Use Euler's method, starting at $x = 0$ with $n = 5$ to estimate the value of $g(5)$.

(a)

2: Correct slope field drawn

(b)

$$\frac{d^2y}{dx^2} = 3x^2 - 4y(x^3 - 2y^2)$$
$$= 3x^2 - 4x^3y + 8y^3$$

In the second quadrant, $x < 0$, and $y > 0$. Therefore $3x^2 - 4x^3y + 8y^3 > 0$ in quadrant II. Solution curves are all concave up.

$3:\begin{cases} 1: \text{Correct second derivative} \\ \quad 1: \text{Correct substitution} \\ \quad 1: \text{Correct answer and} \\ \qquad \text{justification} \end{cases}$

(c)

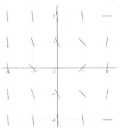

x	$h \cdot f'(x - h)$	$f(x)$ $= f(x-h)$ $+ f'(x-h) \cdot h$
0	-	1
1	-2	$1 - 2 = -1$
2	-1	$-1 - 1 = -2$
3	0	$-2 + 0 = -2$
4	19	$-2 + 19 = 17$
5	-514	-497

$4:\begin{cases} 3: \text{Correct Table Values} \\ \qquad h \\ \qquad f'(x - h) \\ \qquad h \cdot f'(x - h) \\ \quad 1: \text{Answer} \end{cases}$

316

Above is the graph of the parametric curve $r = 4$.

(a) Convert the curve from parametric to Cartesian form.
(b) Find the location(s) on the polar curve where $x = 2$ from $0 \le \theta \le 2\pi$.
(c) This parametric curve is the derivative for the curve $r = 4\theta$. What do the values of $r = 4$ for $0 \le \theta \le 2\pi$ mean for the curve's antiderivative?
(d) Find the area under $r = 4\theta$ from $0 \le \theta \le 2\pi$.
(e) The curve $r = 4\theta$ represents a model for the growth of plants, where the length of r is the growth of the plant in centimeters at a specific day θ. Find the length of a plant growing according to this model 5 days after being planted.

(b) $r = \sqrt{x^2 + y^2}$ $\quad 16 = x^2 + y^2$	1: Correct Cartesian equation
(c) $x = 4\cos(\theta)$ $\theta = \cos^{-1}\left(\dfrac{1}{2}\right) = \dfrac{\pi}{3}, \dfrac{5\pi}{3}$	$2:\begin{cases}1: x = r \cdot \cos(\theta) = 4\cos(\theta) \\ \qquad 1: \text{Answers}\end{cases}$
(d) $r = 4$ is positive for all $\quad 0 \le \theta \le 2\pi$ $\quad r = 4\theta$ is increasing $\quad$ for all $0 \le \theta \le 2\pi$	$2:\begin{cases}1: r = 4 \text{ always positive} \\ 1: r = 4\theta \text{ always increasing}\end{cases}$
(e) $A = \dfrac{1}{2}\int_0^{2\pi}(4\theta)^2 d\theta$ $\quad \left[\dfrac{16}{6}\theta^3\right]_0^{2\pi} = \dfrac{64\pi^3}{3}$	$2:\begin{cases}1: \text{Correct integral} \\ \qquad 1: \text{Answer}\end{cases}$
(f) $L = \int_0^5 \sqrt{(4)^2 + 1}\, d\theta$ $\quad L = 5\sqrt{17}$ cm	$2:\begin{cases}1: \text{Correct integral} \\ 1: \text{Answer with units}\end{cases}$

AP AB/BC Calculus Scoring Guidelines Question 5

A particle moves along the x-axis over time t by the equation below.

$$s(t) = t^3 - 6t^2 - 9t - 18$$

(a) Find the velocity and acceleration functions for the particle.
(b) When is the particle at rest?
(c) When is the particle moving in the forward?
(d) When is the particle increasing in speed?
(e) When is the particle moving the slowest?
(f) Find the total distance travelled by the particle after 5 seconds.

(a) $v(t) = 3t^2 - 12t + 9$ $a(t) = 6t - 12 = 6(t-2)$	$2: \begin{cases} 1: \text{Correct } v(t) \\ 1: \text{Correct } a(t) \end{cases}$
(b) $v(t) = 0 = 3(t-3)(t-1)$ $t = 3, t = 1$	$1: \text{Correct times}$
(c) $v(t)$ is positive when particle moves forward $\quad 0 \le t < 1, 3 < t < \infty$	$2: \begin{cases} 1: v(t) \text{ is positive} \\ 1: \text{Correct time ranges} \end{cases}$
(d) Both $v(t)$ and $a(t)$ must have same sign. $1 < t < 2$ Both negative $3 < t < \infty$ Both positive	$1: \text{Correct time ranges}$
(e) $a(t) = v'(t)$ $a(t) = 0, t = 2$ Critical Point $a(t)$ changes from negative to positive about $t = 2$, therefore $t = 2$ is a local minimum on $v(t)$	$1: \text{Local min with justification}$
(f) $\text{Distance} = \displaystyle\int_0^5 |v(t)| dt$ $\displaystyle\int_0^5 v(t)dt - 2\int_1^3 v(t)dt$ $\qquad = 28 \; units$	$2: \begin{cases} 1: \text{Correct integrals} \\ \quad 1: \text{Answer} \end{cases}$

AP Calculus BC Scoring Guidelines Question 6

Consider the following Maclaurin series for the function f.

$$\sum_{n=1}^{\infty} \frac{(-2)^{n+1}}{n+1} x^n = 2x - \frac{8}{3}x^2 + 4x^3 + \cdots \frac{(-2)^{n+1}}{n+1} x^n + \cdots$$

(a) Use the ratio test to determine the radius and interval of convergence for the series above.

(b) Write the first three nonzero terms of the Maclaurin series for F, the antiderivative of f. Then find the power series F.

(c) Write the first three nonzero terms of the Maclaurin series for $\cos(x)$. Use this series to write the third degree Maclaurin polynomial for $h(x) = \cos(x) f(x)$.

(a) $\lim\limits_{n \to \infty} \left| \dfrac{(-2)^{n+2} x^{n+1}}{n+2} \cdot \dfrac{n+1}{(-2)^{n+1} x^n} \right|$

$|x| < \dfrac{1}{2}, R = \dfrac{1}{2}$

$-\dfrac{1}{2} < x < \dfrac{1}{2}$

Test $x = -\dfrac{1}{2}$

$\dfrac{(-2)^{n+1}}{n+1}\left(-\dfrac{1}{2}\right)^n$

Diverges by n-th term test

Test $x = \dfrac{1}{2}$

$\dfrac{(-2)^{n+1}}{n+1}\left(\dfrac{1}{2}\right)^n$

Converges by alt. series test

Interval of Convergence

$= \left(-\dfrac{1}{2}, \dfrac{1}{2}\right]$

$4: \begin{cases} 1: \text{Correct application} \\ \quad \text{of ratio test} \\ 1: \text{Correct interval} \\ 1: \text{Testing of endpoints} \\ 1: \text{Answers} \end{cases}$

(Any test can be used to evaluate convergence or divergence of endpoints)

(b) First three terms:

$$x^2 - \frac{8}{9}x^3 + x^4$$

$$F = \sum_{n=1}^{\infty} \frac{(-2)^{n+1}}{(n+1)^2} x^{(n+1)}$$

(c)

$$\cos(x) = 1 - \frac{x^2}{2} + \frac{x^4}{24} + \cdots$$

$$f(x) = 2x - \frac{8}{3}x^2 + 4x^3 + \cdots$$

$$h(x) = \left[1 - \frac{x^2}{2} + \frac{x^4}{24} + \cdots\right]$$

$$\cdot \left[2x - \frac{8}{3}x^2 + 4x^3 + \cdots\right] = \left(2x - \frac{8}{3}x^2 + 3x^3 + \cdots\right)$$

$$2: \begin{cases} 1: \text{Correct terms} \\ 1: \text{Correct power series} \end{cases}$$

$$3: \begin{cases} 1: \text{Correct series for } \cos(x) \\ 1: \text{Correct multiplication} \\ 1: \text{Answer} \end{cases}$$

Made in United States
North Haven, CT
02 December 2023

44909370R00183